SAN FRANCISCO
Chinatown

A Guide to Its History
and Architecture

Philip P. Choy

Architectural Photographs
by Brian W. Choy

City Lights • San Francisco

Library of Congress Cataloging-in-Publication Data

Choy, Philip P.
 San Francisco Chinatown : a guide to its history and
architecture / Philip P. Choy.
    p. cm.
 ISBN 978-0-87286-540-2
1. Chinatown (San Francisco, Calif.)—Tours. 2. Chinatown (San Francisco, Calif.)—History. 3. Chinatown (San
Francisco, Calif.)—Description and travel. 4. Chinese
Americans—California—San Francisco. 5. Historic sites—
California—San Francisco. 6. San Francisco (Calif.)—Tours.
7. San Francisco (Calif.)—History. 8. San Francisco (Calif.)—Description and travel. I. Title.

 F869.S36C4717 2012
 979.4'61—dc23

                                    2012012592

City Lights Books are published at the City Lights Bookstore
261 Columbus Avenue, San Francisco, CA 94133
www.citylights.com

This book is dedicated to the late Him Mark Lai,
Dean of Chinese American History.

CONTENTS

PREFACE

From the time of the Gold Rush of 1849 to the present, Chinatown has been a "must-see" in every guidebook on San Francisco. Chinatown in the 19th century was singled out as a blight on the urban landscape of the city, its infamous reputation spreading to the far corners of the nation. Visitors were warned not to wander alone but were advised instead to hire licensed guides for safety. Only the guides could take you through the maze of secret underground tunnels into the bowels of the earth, where you could witness a "peculiar" race dwelling in darkness.

Descriptions of a mysterious Chinese quarter were so compelling that John W. Wilson, a young man from a small village east of Indianapolis who joined the army during the Boxer Rebellion, returned home via San Francisco, determined to see Chinatown. In an oral history taken in 1969 by Thomas Krasean of the Indiana Historical Society, Wilson recalled his experience.

JW: And I come over to Frisco and we all wanted to see Chinatown, there was ten of us. So Chinatown was underground at that time, you know ... City underneath. Did you never read about that? Boy, beat anything you ever saw in your life.

TK: Actually underground, you mean?

JW: Actually underground, business houses ... opium dens and everything else down in under there. Well, we were standing in front of this agency waiting for a guide ... there

> was a Chinaman walked up . . . and said, "I
> am a guide. . . ." Well we hired him. We got
> underground and we went in a saloon . . .
> down a stairway and then . . . he says, "Now,
> you are underground. . . ."

The remainder of the interview tells how the guide, who held the only torchlight, vanished and left them wandering in the dark. While desperately searching for a way out, Wilson's friend nearly stepped through a trap door and if he had fallen through, he might never have been heard from again. According to Wilson, this was the way people were robbed. After their horrifying experience, he and his friend finally found their way out in the morning. The rest didn't get out until later that evening.

John Wilson continued:

> But everybody had a different experience from
> the other fellow . . . wandering around, told
> they get into . . . opium dens and everything
> else, you know. Underground . . . that was
> underground before the earthquake. When the
> earthquake . . . thousands of people died under
> there that nobody ever known about.

These images of an infamous Chinatown began to change after the 1906 Earthquake. Guides applying for licenses issued by the police commission were warned not to refabricate and promote the evil spectacle of an underground Chinatown, lest their licenses be revoked. Public opinion began to improve, aided by a series of positive articles run by the *San Francisco Chronicle*. The Chinese also promoted this improvement by planning a new Oriental City.

Today, inspired by the Civil Rights Movement of the '60s and '70s, the social pendulum has swung toward the appreciation of ethnic and cultural diversity. Chinatown is now singled out as an asset to the urban landscape of the city. Thousands come to visit the same 19th century "exotic heathen temples" with neither disdain nor contempt but with intellectual curiosity, to dine with the locals where once no white man dared to eat the strange odoriferous food. Case in point: when the *San Francisco Chronicle* on April 20th reported the closing of Sam Wo's Restaurant, a dirty, rickety, narrow, three-story, one-hundred-year-old hole in the wall condemned by Public Health for conditions unsuitable for the preparation and storage of food, a block-long line of old-time Chinese and non-Chinese customers waited to enjoy a final meal there. Each spring when the parade dragon rears its magnificent golden head, thousands of visitors pack into Chinatown, fascinated with the appearance of a nonassimilated foreign community complete with exotic cultural traditions.

The treatment of Chinatown both in the past and in the present obscures the reality of history. Few realize that the existence of the community is intimately interwoven with the history of the city. The intent of this guidebook is to place the evolution of the Chinese community in the context of the U.S./China relationship and reclaim our rightful place in the annals of America.

ACKNOWLEDGMENTS

It has been a pleasure to work with Garrett Caples, who submitted my manuscript for publication, and Linda Ronan and Jolene Torr of City Lights Books.

I wish to thank Lil Jew for sharing her knowledge of Cantonese operas, Kevin Wong for providing me with articles on his dad, "Woo Woo" Wong, Richard Everett for digging up the 1930 article on the Calaveras County Chinese prefab courthouse, and Dr. Collin Quock for information on the Chinese Hospital.

In all my projects promoting knowledge of the Chinese of America, I have been blessed with the assistance of family members. I'm indebted to my grandchildren, Alexandria Choy and Nathan Wong, and Nathan's friend Joanna Ho, for spending weeks during summer break from college in 2011, scanning microfilm articles from the library; Jia Wen Wei for being on the spot when I needed help navigating the computer; daughter Stephanie for reading my manuscript to insure that I not loose sight of objectivity by injecting my biases. The photographs of the buildings were taken in 1980 by my son Brian for a case report to nominate Chinatown as a historic district. For months, he was a lone figure on the streets at the early hour of 6:00 a.m., in order to avoid the vehicular and pedestrian traffic and photograph the buildings without obstruction. Finally, a loving appreciation to my wife Sarah of the IBM Selectric generation, who, braving the complexity of the computer, typed and retyped the manuscript.

Philip P. Choy, 4/26/12

INTRODUCTION

The arrival of the Chinese in the United States toward the end of the 1840s was part of an intricate political and economic relationship between Asia and America.

From its birth as a nation, the United States sought to establish itself as a new power among old nations. Many Americans believed in the concept of "Manifest Destiny," which held that the United States had the right to expand westward across the continent to the Pacific Ocean. The West Coast would be the gateway through which America would acquire and hold the positions of power in Asia.

On the West Coast, in California, San Francisco became not only a major commercial port but also the main port of entry for Chinese immigrants, who were recruited as a source of mass labor for the economic development of the western frontier. Initially, white Americans welcomed Chinese participation in San Francisco's civic events, such as the celebration, at Portsmouth Square, of California's admission into the Union in 1850. At the time, the Square was the heart of San Francisco. However, while the City expanded, the Chinese stayed in the area. For over a century and a half, Chinatown has remained in this same location.

The interaction between Chinatown and the community at large has not always been one of mutual understanding. Caught in the struggle between the white laboring class fighting for better working conditions and the industrial capitalists seeking to maintain the status quo, the Chinese became scapegoats for the growing pains of the American labor movement in the West. Sinophobia in the 19th century echoed into the 20th century with the cry "The Chinese must go!" The question of Chinese labor competition occupied a central place in the Nation's politics for over 30 years, until the passage of the Exclusion Act of May 1882, which in effect closed the door to Chinese immigration.

From time to time, San Francisco attempted to destroy Chinatown and remove the Chinese through both legal and extralegal means. The Chinese responded strategically. When the Board of Supervisors attempted to remove Chinatown after the Earthquake of 1906, for example, the Chinese strove to earn the goodwill of the City by creating a new positive image, retaining architects to transform the neighborhood slums into an "Oriental City." This new trend of a Sino-architectural vernacular, created specifically as a response to the threat of relocation after the quake, shaped the present skyline of Chinatown.

But Chinatown has always been a tourist attraction. What was sensationalized in the 19th century as a haven for racial peculiarities and cultural oddities is perceived today as an ethnic enclave where cultural habits and traditions are preserved. In either case, the stereotypical image of Chinatown as an unassimilated foreign community remains unchanged. But the significance of Chinatown lies not in cultural exotics. Beneath the Oriental façade is a history rooted in the political past of the City, the State, and the Nation.

That history began following our War for Independence in 1776. The evidence is before our eyes and under our noses if we know what to look for as we tour Chinatown. Tea, ginseng, and the churches take us back to when two peoples of diverse cultures first met, traded, and interacted. In 1784, when Samuel Shaw sailed the first American ship, the *Empress of China*, into Bocca Tigrus, he traded twenty-eight tons of ginseng and 20,000 Spanish dollars for tea, silk, porcelain, and other treasures. In his journal, Shaw wrote: "The inhabitants of America must have tea . . . that useless produce [ginseng] of her mountains and forest will supply her with this elegant luxury . . . such are the advantages which America derives from her ginseng" (Quincy 1847, 231). That historic voyage began our interest in the Far East and subsequently led to frontiersmen's hunting and trapping off the California coast for the pelts of sea otters for the Canton market. When gold was discovered, the transpacific commerce between California and Canton (now called "Guangzhou") continued, not only with the importation of Chinese goods for the Gold Rush population but also with the arrival of Chinese laborers from the Pearl River Delta, centered on the City of Canton in Guangdong Province.

From the time of their first encounter in the 16th century, Western nations were determined to open China's ports to trade. Equally stubborn, China called herself the "Middle Kingdom" (i.e., the center of the world) and attempted to close her doors to the "uncivilized, meddling, barbarians." By the time of Shaw's arrival, China had been conquered by the Manchu from Manchuria, who ruled under the title "Ching" (brilliance) from 1644 to 1911. The Manchu adopted Chinese ways and appointed collaborators in government posts to maintain control over the population. After two and a half centuries, the Manchu had been absorbed into Chinese culture, except for the Manchu style of dress and the shaven head with the queue (pigtail), which were forced upon the Chinese as symbols of subjugation.

In 1757, the Manchu Emperor Chien Lung (1736-1796) restricted all foreign trade to one port, the City of Canton. Trading between the Chinese and Europeans was controlled and regulated by Chinese merchants known as Hong, authorized by the Imperial government. Unfair practices, import and export taxes, and the demand for silver in payment for goods created trade deficits among foreign nations doing business in China. To offset the deficits, these nations smuggled opium into China in large quantities. The British, whose merchants had control of the supply from India, dominated the trade. American merchants obtained their supply from Smyrna, Turkey. China's attempts to stop the smuggling resulted in war with Great Britain (1839-1842). The British easily defeated China and forced its government to open the ports of Canton, Shanghai, Ningpo, Amoy, and Foochow. In addition, the territory of Hong Kong was ceded to England for 100 years.

In the last quarter of the 18th century, glowing accounts published on the exploration and adventures in the South Seas, India, and Africa, not only

Dr. Morrison translating the Bible with Chinese converts, 1820.

fired the imagination and curiosity of the public but also aroused the evangelical impulse of Protestant leaders, who founded missionary boards and societies to recruit and send missionaries into the heathen world. While British and American merchants opened the doors to the treasures of "Cathay" (China), European and American missionaries envisioned opening the door to the Kingdom of God for China's three hundred million "heathens." This missionary enterprise was a part of the Christian revivalist movement known as the "Second Great Awakening."

At the beginning of the 19th century, this Protestant religious movement led to the founding of the London Missionary Society (LMS), followed by the founding of the American Board of Commissions of Foreign Missions (ABCFM). In 1807, the LMS sent The Reverend Robert Morrison to China and, in 1830, the ABCFM sent The Reverend David Abeel and The Reverend Elijah Bridgman. Canton became the staging area for Protestant missionary activities. These religious activities, together with the long period of commerce with China, promoted knowledge of the West in China, and linked Canton to California. To the Westerner, the Chinese from Canton were known as "Cantonese." These were the Chinese who would set foot in California when gold was discovered.

Leaders of the evangelical movement quickly realized the strategic importance of California lay not only in the fact that it fronted the Pacific, but also in the unique missionary opportunity the presence of thousands of Chinese afforded; if converted, these Cantonese people could return home to spread the gospel to the teeming millions in China who had never heard the revelation of God. Thus, the many churches in Chinatown today are the result of the efforts of the early Christian pioneers begun in Canton, Macau, and Hong Kong. In San Francisco, the first official evangelical effort took place in a public ceremony on August 28, 1850, when Mayor John Geary and The Reverend Albert Williams invited the Chinese residents to Portsmouth Square to receive religious tracts that were printed in Chinese and published in Canton.

But the fascination with which the West viewed China in the 18th century deteriorated to disre-

American tea clipper Nightingale, *breaking through the China coast.*

spect and disdain by the 19th century. Following its defeat in the Opium War with England, China under the Manchu rulers was on the verge of collapse. Unable to deal with the belligerent demands of Western powers, the government adopted a foreign policy of appeasement, granting concession after concession. Foreign exploitation, internal rebellion, and overpopulation accelerated the decline of China's economy and the deterioration of social conditions.

At the same time, the efforts of the Second Great Awakening that had brought Protestant evangelists to China also hastened the end of the African slave trade, creating a worldwide shortage of cheap labor. The Chinese from Guangdong Province filled this void. American and British ships carried human cargo under wretched conditions throughout Southeast Asia, Cuba, Hawaii, the

Chincha Islands in Peru, and Mauritius and Madagascar off the coast of Africa. This same cheap labor was the resource by which California was developed.

Present-day Chinatown overlays significant sites from different periods of San Francisco's history: the Spanish period, the Mexican period, and the American period.

Spanish Period (1776-1821)

In 1769, the Spanish government sent Don Gaspar Portola and Father Junipera Serra to claim California for Spain by establishing a system of missions intended to prevent British and Russian intrusion. British and Russian interest in California had been triggered by the successful voyage of Captain James Cook into the South Seas, when the crew discovered the tremendous profits to be made from selling fur in Canton. Along the Pacific Coast, sea otter was found in abundance, and the skin of a mature otter brought a price as high as three hundred dollars. In the late 18th century, when New England merchants learned of this lucrative market, American interest in California began.

On June 17, 1776, Lt. Jose Joaquin Moraga of Spain led an expedition of soldiers and their families to the San Francisco Bay Area. They established the Presidio on September 17th and the Mission Dolores on October 9th. Lt. Moraga took charge of the Presidio and Father Francisco Palou and Father Cambon were responsible for the Mission. For decades the only social life was between families at the Mission and Presidio, together known as "Yerba Buena" from the herb of that name that grew along the road between the settlements. Except for occasional sailors from ships anchored on the bay for supplies, there was little connection to the outside world.

Mexican Period (1821-1848)

In 1821, General Augustin de Iturbide declared Mexico's independence from Spain and California entered a period of Mexican rule. A year later, the British whaler *Orion* sailed into San Francisco Bay. While on shore, members of the crew enjoyed the hospitality of Ignazio Martinez and the families at the Presidio. When the *Orion* sailed off, Chief Mate William A. Richardson remained behind. Whether Richardson deserted the ship because of Maria Antonia, whom he met during the festivities, is not known, but three years later they were married. Richardson became a Mexican citizen and, because of his knowledge of navigation, he was appointed harbormaster and granted a plot of land. In 1832, he built an adobe house for his family, fronting the west side of Calle de la Fondacion (now 823 Grant Avenue). One year later, in December 1833, Jacob Leese, an American who came to California from Ohio, built a house on the same road, two hundred feet south of Richardson (now the southwest corner of Clay and Grant). Like Richardson, Leese became a Mexican citizen and married a Spanish lady, the sister of Salvador Vallejo.

The families of Richardson and Leese were the only households between the Mission and Presidio. Reminiscing on his trip entering the Bay, Richard Henry Dana, Jr., the author of *Two Years Before the Mast* wrote: "It was in the winter of 1835-36 that the ship *Alert* in prosecution of her voyage for hides on the remote and almost unknown coast of California, floated into the vast solitude of the bay of San Francisco; all around was stillness of nature."

That "stillness of nature" would be interrupted forever in the next decade when America became interested in annexation of California and when gold was discovered on the American River.

American Period (1846-Present)

A half-century of contact with California—originating with the sea otter trade among Boston, California, and Canton, and followed by the New England hide and tallow trade—laid the foundation for American interest in California and sparked American expansion westward as her Manifest Destiny. Both President Andrew Jackson and President John Tyler saw the importance of annexing California, not only for its desirable ports for whaling vessels but also for the potential dominance of trade across the Pacific.

When President James K. Polk assumed office in March 1845, he was determined to annex California either by purchase, by encouraging California to revolt against Mexican rule, or as a last resort, by war with Mexico. War it was! On July 7, 1846 Commodore John D. Sloat raised the United States flag at Montgomery and proclaimed California part of the United States. No one was there to surrender. A message was sent to Captain Montgomery in San Francisco and on July 9, 1846, the American flag was hoisted on the square. John Henry Brown gave this eyewitness account:

> On the following day, shortly before noon, we heard the fife and the beating of the drum. There was great rejoicing by the few who were

San Francisco, November 1948.

in the city, and the small and faithful band
were as united as brothers, and their hearts
swelled with pure pride and patriotism at the
thoughts of being under the protection of
the flag of their country. The first person who
made his appearance was Captain Watson of
the marines, with his company of soldiers. The
next in command was the First Lieutenant of
the Portsmouth. He was followed by Lieutenant Revere's two Mid-shipmen, and about a
dozen sailors. They all marched up Clay Street
to Kearny, and thence to the Old Mexican flag
pole in front of the Adobe House, used as a
Custom House. This being an important event
in the History of San Francisco, I will give
the names of those who witnessed the hoist-
ing of the American Flag: Captain Leidsoff,
John Finch, Joseph Thompson, Mrs. Robert
T. Ridley, Mrs. Andrew Hepner, Mrs. Captain
Voight, Richard the Third, and John H. Brown.

San Francisco, November 1949.

The war ended on February 2, 1848, with the signing of the Treaty of Guadalupe Hidalgo. The terms of the treaty called for the United States to annex the territories of California and Texas in exchange for a $15-million payment to Mexico. Nine days earlier, on January 24, 1848, James Wilson Marshall had discovered gold on the American River, but California now belonged to the United States.

Marshall had contracted with John A. Sutter to build a sawmill at Coloma and while inspecting the work, discovered particles of gold in the riverbed. After ascertaining the specimens were actually gold, Marshall and Sutter agreed to keep the discovery a secret. But their efforts to keep the news from spreading proved impossible. When Samuel Brannan, who ran a general store at Sutter Fort, learned of the discovery, he quietly cornered the market on every type of mining equipment and then on May 12, 1848, appeared excitedly at Portsmouth Square shouting: "Gold! gold! from the American River!" The secret was out and the world rushed in.

San Francisco emerged from a sleepy trading port of three hundred at the time Marshall discovered gold to a bustling town of two thousand at the beginning of 1849; by the end of that year, the population had exploded to over 25,000. People of all occupations, professions, colors, and creeds mingled at the Square, gambling and drinking at surrounding saloons. While legendary bartender Professor Jerry Thomas concocted his famous cocktail, "Tom & Jerry" (Asbury 1938, 22), on one side of the Square, Reverend Taylor was preaching his sermon "The Way of the Transgressor Is Hard" on the other. Passersby paid little heed to the preacher as their "way" was to "Little Chile," the red-light district of the time, or to Madame Ah Toy's brothel on Clay Street; if the lines were too long, they could go further up the hill to Cora Bell on Pike Street (now Waverly Place).

It was customary for people to settle within their own ethnic communities. Mexicans, Peruvians, and Chileans settled in "Little Chile" on the northern end of Kearny at the foot of Pacific and Broadway. Germans and French occupied the southern end of Kearny. The Chinese settled on Sacramento Street The Germans formed the German Benevolent Society and the French formed their own French Benevolent Society. Likewise, Chinese coming from different geographic areas around the Pearl River Delta in Guangdong formed their own organizations called *hui kuan*. Though initially rivals, the various *hui kuan* would eventually band together as the Chinese Six Companies—later known as the Chinese Consolidated Benevolent Association—

serving an important leadership role in the Chinese community.

Chinatown Beginnings

The first known person of Chinese descent to settle in San Francisco was a woman. On February 2, 1848, nine days after Marshall's discovery of gold, an American merchant, Charles Van Gillespie, and his wife arrived from Hong Kong on the *Brig Eagle*, with two Chinese male servants and a Chinese maid named Maria Seise. The two men disappeared into the gold fields but Maria stayed with the Gillespies for thirty years. Shortly after the Trinity Episcopal Church was organized on July 22, 1849, Mrs. Sarah Catherine Gillespie and Maria Seise were among the first to be confirmed by Bishop Inghram. The Gillespies settled on the southeast corner of Dupont and Washington Street, where Mrs. Gillespie started the first Sunday school in San Francisco.

When Mr. Gillespie arrived in San Francisco, he brought a shipment of goods from China. He placed an ad on April 1, 1848, in Sam Brannan's *California Star*, and his goods were quickly sold. It was Gillespie's intention to introduce Chinese laborers as well as goods to the rapidly developing California. The idea was not new. Earlier American merchants had planned to use Chinese laborers in California. In a letter dated October 7, 1837, Nathan Spear in Monterey requested of William C. Little, merchant in the China Trade, to procure for him one carpenter, two shoemakers, one baker, one cook, and one steward from Canton. As the dis-

Imports from China.

covery of gold opened the floodgates to immigration and commerce, Chinese immigrants began to fill the need for domestics and laborers in the new frontier. Embarking from the Atlantic States, ships would sail around the Horn of South America, cross the Pacific to Canton, and return carrying hundreds of Chinese laborers and cargoes of Chinese goods. China goods included fancy bedsteads, lounges, chairs with tables and other furniture, silk, shawls, ivory work, and stoneware, enough to supply the burgeoning city. For example, against the wall of the dormitory on the third floor of the J. L. Riddle & Co. store were large China water jars, China washstands and China stone washbasins, and coconut shell dippers (Barry and Patten 1947, 100).

Hundreds of imported Chinese prefabricated wooden houses added to the City's housing inventory. Bayard Taylor, a journalist for the *New York Tribune*, reported that at least seventy-five houses imported from Canton were put up by Chinese carpenters. On his way to visit Colonel John C. Fremont in Happy Valley (around Second and Market Streets), Mr. Taylor reported he saw a company of Chinese carpenters putting up the frame of a Canton-made house. Upon arrival, Taylor was greeted

The remains of the first Calaveras County Courthouse in Double Springs, originally created by placing two Chinese prefab houses in tandem.

by Colonel Fremont in his own Chinese house. Etienne Derbec, a French journalist, reported that the Chinese houses were available in either European or Celestial Empire styles and gave his opinion that they were the prettiest, the best made, and the cheapest local dwellings. In 1851, John Frost, author of *Pictorial History of California*, wrote that these houses "were infinitely superior and more substantial than those erected by the Yankees. . . ." Apart from these brief descriptions by early writers, however, little was known about these structures until 1990, when archaeologist Professor Thomas N. Layton found a bill of lading for a complete prefabricated house in the ship *Frolic*, wrecked on the Mendocino Coast in the winter of 1850 on her return voyage from China. Further investigation led to Double Spring Ranch, Calaveras County and the discovery of two Chinese houses in tandem formerly used as the Calaveras County courthouse and later as the County post office. Part of this building has been restored and is now displayed at the Cala-veras County Museum.

As city service improvements expanded beyond Portsmouth Square, brick and stone buildings were built on California, Sansome, Battery, and Mont-gomery Streets. The lower stories of these buildings were often constructed of imported Chinese gran-ite. As early as 1852, a prefabricated stone building was erected at the northwest corner of Montgomery and California Streets. A crew of Chinese masons under contract with the owner, John Parrot, erected the building. Each stone was marked to instruct the workers how to assemble the structure.

Even as the Chinese moved about the City among the polyglot population, there was a sense they were strangers in a strange land. As if they had premonition of the difficult times to come, on the evening of November 19, 1849, four leading mer-chants of the community, Ahi, Jon-Ling, Atung, and Attoon, led some three hundred Chinese resi-dents to the Canton Restaurant on Jackson Street to retain the services of Selim E. Woodsworth, Esq. to act as arbitrator and counselor "in the event of unforeseen difficulties wherein we should be at a loss as to what cause of action it might be necessary for us to pursue." Hon. J. W. Geary—who governed the city as its last "alcade" under the old Spanish municipal system and its first mayor following Cal-ifornia's admission to statehood—and other public dignitaries attended the affair and commended the action.

The "China Boys," as the local Chinese resi-dents referred to themselves, were a familiar scene on the Square, where they participated in civic celebrations on Admission Day, Washington's Birthday, and Independence Day. Their fancy, colorful embroidered silk and satin clothing never failed to dazzle the spectators and prompted the *California Courier* to print: "We have never seen a finer looking body of men collected together in San Francisco. In fact, this portion of our population is a pattern of sobriety, order and obedience to laws . . . not only to other residents but to Americans themselves." Likewise, in regards to the arrival of the Chinese, the *Alta California* wrote on May 13, 1851, "scarcely a ship arrives here that does not bring an increase to this worthy integer of our population . . . the Chinese Boys will yet vote at the same polls, study at the same schools and bow at the same altar as our own countrymen."

Such platitudes, however, proved wrong. Even as the press predicted that the Chinese will "yet vote at our polls," the premonition of difficult times was to come true. On December 29, 1854, Judge John Satterlee denied a Chinese application for citizenship on the basis that he did not belong to the Caucasian race. Earlier that same year, in *People v. Hall* (4 Cal.399), Chief Justice Hugh C. Murray of the California Supreme Court ruled that the Act of April 16, 1850, Section 14, which forbade "Blacks and Indians" from testifying in favor of or against a white man, was applicable to the Chinese, who were legally Indians because both groups were descended from the same Asiatic ancestors. The opinion of Supreme Court Justice C.J. Murray was: "When Columbus first landed upon the shores of this continent . . . he imagined that he had accomplished the object of his expedition, and that the Island of San Salvador was one of those islands of the Chinese Sea lying near the extremity of India. . . . Acting upon the hypothesis, he gave to the Islanders the name Indian. From that time . . . the American Indian and the Mongolian or Asiatic, were regarded as the same type of human species." These legal decisions would lead to open hostility and violence in the gold mining districts of California.

As newer residential and business districts developed in San Francisco, the old section was abandoned to the Chinese. During the period of the Civil War, which prevented importation of manufactured goods from the Eastern United States and stimulated expansion of light industry in the West, Chinatown became a light industrial center. Buildings were converted to accommodate the production of cigars, clothing, and shoes. For example, the Globe on the northwest corner of Jackson and Dupont, which at one time was one of San Francisco's finest hotels, was converted to a cigar factory on one floor, a house for prostitution on another, and a school for children on the ground floor. (City planners of today did not invent multi-use buildings!) But this expansion into business was met with alarm and resentment. The *San Francisco Chronicle* on July 21, 1878, described the Chinese expansion as the "Mongolian octopus fastening its tentacles around the City." Henry George, a reporter for the *New York Tribune*, wrote on May 1, 1869: "the Chinese are rapidly monopolizing employment in all the lighter branches of industry . . . such as running sewing machines; making paper boxes and bags, binding shoes, labeling and packing machines, etc. They are acting as firemen upon steamers; running stationary engines, painting carriages, upholstering furniture; making boots, shoes and clothing, cigars, tin, and woodenware."

Anti-Chinese Politics

The economic depression in the East that followed the Civil War was not felt in California until the 1870s. A steady stream of unemployed Easterners took advantage of the first transcontinental railroad—completed in 1869 with the help of over 12,000 Chinese laborers—to come to California, attracted by its depiction as a land of prosperity in advertisements created by pro-business organizations and land speculators. The California Labor and Employment Exchange and the Immigrant Aid Association used such advertisements to draw labor from the East, seeking to flood the market with laborers in order to combat the demands of unionism in California.

In the late nineteenth century, conflict between employers and laborers dominated the political landscape, with the Chinese caught in the middle as scapegoats. The workingmen's struggle for an eight-hour day, for mechanics' lien laws, against convict labor, and especially against the monopoly of the railroads, degenerated into anti-Chinese hysteria. Laborers cursed the Big Four, they cursed pro-Chinese advocates, but they physically attacked the Chinese. For over three decades the battle cry was "The Chinese must go!"—a phrase coined by a

Dehumanizing carcatures of the Chinese compounded Sinophobic hysteria.

demagogue, Denis Kearney, leader of the Workingmen's Party of California. He and his partner Dr. C. C. O'Donnell incited mobs at sandlot meetings. As O'Donnell said on October 25, 1877: "We are going to march to the Pacific Mail Docks and . . . not . . . allow any more Chinese to be landed . . . and if they persist . . . the Association will blow their ships out of the water" (*Call* 11/6/77). Likewise, Kearny threatened: "We have men who will manufacture balloons for dropping dynamite into Chinatown."

San Francisco was outraged at Chinese labor competition and took circuitous routes to outlaw or tax Chinese businesses. San Francisco's Board of Supervisors, for example, passed ordinances that impacted only the Chinese. One ordinance forbade merchants from carrying laundry, vegetable baskets, and other wares on shoulder poles. Laundries that operated with a one-horse vehicle were taxed one dollar, while Chinese laundries that carried laundry by hand were taxed $15.00. Another ordinance, aimed at the practice of bunk-bed lodging in Chinatown, outlawed sleeping in any room with less than 500 cubic feet per person. When the Chinese packed the jails instead of paying their fine for these violations, another ordinance was passed to cut off their queues, in an attempt to humiliate the dissenters.

Far from being a fringe viewpoint, Kearney's Workingmen's Party had a powerful influence on mainstream society. The new State Constitution, for example, drafted with the Party's input and enacted in 1879, gave cities and towns "all necessary power . . . of this State for the removal of Chinese. . . ." This section of the Constitution would not be removed until November 4, 1952. But there was a major federal obstacle to the execution of this state power, and the anti-Chinese movement more generally: the Burlingame Treaty between China and the United States. Earlier treaties between the two nations in 1844 and 1858 gave the United States and its citizens unilateral privileges of trade and commerce with China. In the interest of continuing trade and missionary activities, the Burlingame Treaty of 1868 pledged reciprocal immigration between the two countries. The passage of this treaty was opposed bitterly by California as opening the gates to the "hordes" of Chinese who would drive out white labor.

Protests from the Pacific Coast poured into Congress, seeking action to prevent Chinese im-

Mass anti-Chinese meetings incited riots.

migration. In response, Congress amended the Burlingame Treaty with the Treaty of 1880 to give the United States the right to regulate the immigration or residence of Chinese laborers; in return, Chinese residing in the United States would be given special protection. This arrangement paved the way for the passage of the Exclusion Act of 1882, which for ten years prohibited the immigration of Chinese laborers. On paper, the Exclusion Act exempted merchants and their families, teachers, diplomats, students, and travelers, but in practice, the law attempted to thwart all Chinese immigration. Over the following decade, residence requirements were stiffened. Under the Geary Act of 1882, the Chinese laborers had to go through a process of registration, and deportations were relentlessly pursued. San Francisco was not satisfied even when all Chinese exclusion acts were extended in 1902 and made "permanent" in 1904.

Equally persistent, the Chinese attempted to

Under the Exclusion Acts, merchants were allowed to immigrate.

immigrate by circumventing the exclusion laws through extralegal means. Inclusion of merchants in the exempt classification was necessary to honor the trade and commercial provisions in the treaties between the United States and China. Through purchasing or claiming partnership in a business firm, a person established himself as a merchant. A merchant's wife and minor children could also immigrate. Because all children of American citizens are citizens by birth, even if born in a foreign country, purchasing the birthright and adopting the identity of a son or daughter of a merchant or a United States citizen became a popular means of immigration. These fraudulent bureaucratic practices became known as the "paper son" racket. Many Chinese also took advantage of the 1906 Earthquake to claim their birth certificates were burned in the fire.

In order to deny admission to the immigrants, immigration officials devised an interrogation system to entrap and expose fraudulent attempts. From 1910 to 1941, the center for housing and processing the new arrivals was located at the Immigration Station on Angel Island. Detainment took anywhere from a few days to a record of two years! Poems carved on the barracks wall by detainees are testaments to their anxiety, fears, frustrations, and disillusionment.

Before the 1906 Earthquake, various proposals were made to reclaim Chinatown. In February 1905, spokesman John Partridge for the United States Improvement and Investment Company boasted, "the City would be relieved of the continual menace. . . ." However, such plans would soon be thwarted by the Earthquake.

Earthquake

On Wednesday, April 18, 1906, at 5:12 a.m., a massive temblor, 8.3 by today's Richter scale, shocked San Francisco, sending thousands of panic-stricken people stumbling into the streets half-dazed and half-dressed. The 48 seconds that shook the earth seemed an eternity. But the worst was yet to come, as fires raged over parts of the city. The City's 585 firemen raced their teams of horses to the sites, hooked up hoses, and started pumping, only to realize—no water! The tremor had ruptured water lines from reservoirs that supplied the City; the underground water mains from cisterns were sheared apart. Assistant Fire Chief Dougherty concluded the only way to check the raging flames and save the City was to dynamite the buildings. Barrels of black powder came from the Presidio military base

The Great Earthquake and Fire, San Francisco, 1906. Looking down California Street from Nob Hill.

and dynamite came from Fort McDowell on Angel Island. Inexperienced soldiers began blowing up buildings under the supervision of a handful of military explosive experts. But the strategy of blowing up buildings ahead of the firestorm in order to create firebreaks instead sent flaming debris into neighboring blocks, starting new fires. Thousands of residents assisting policemen and firemen rescued the trapped and injured and searched for the missing, while hundreds of criminals and greedy civilians looted stores and buildings.

Mayor Eugene Schmitz, heretofore facing criminal and corruption charges with mentor Abe Ruef and the complete Board of Supervisors, rose to the occasion and gallantly took command, as a decent mayor should. He immediately drafted a proclamation authorizing federal troops and the police to shoot and kill all looters. Unfortunately, greed overcame "duty to protect," as some soldiers were among the looters. Ignoring his corrupt political partners, he summoned the leading citizens and

Chinese in segregated relief camp.

organized the "Committee of Fifty" to govern the chaotic city; the committee included two subcommittees, one to designate a location for a segregated relief camp, the other to designate a site for the relocation of Chinatown.

Another major figure who took charge of the City was General Frederick Funston, Deputy Commander of the Presidio; he deployed 1700 of his troops into the City, supporting firemen and police wherever help was most urgently needed. Soldiers with fixed bayonets were posted everywhere to discourage looting. Under his orders blocks of buildings were dynamited ahead of flaming buildings. In effect, martial law was unofficially declared.

After four days of firefighting and dynamiting, an area east of Van Ness to the waterfront and south of Market to north of the Bay was a ruin of smoldering ashes. Within the burnt area, old Chinatown was gone forever.

Architect Clarence R. Ward's proposal for the southwest corner of Wahsington and Grant Streets.

Chinatown Post-Quake

On April 23rd, the subcommittee to relocate Chinatown proposed to move Chinatown to Hunters Point. However, the Chinese had plans of their own. Even before the 1906 Earthquake, while San Francisco was entertaining David Burnham's master plan for a new city, Look Tin Eli, secretary of the Chinese Chamber of Commerce, and other prominent merchants including Tong Bong and Lew Hing conjured visions of a new "Oriental City" to give greater San Francisco "veritable fairy palaces filled with the choicest treasures of the Orient. . . ." While the City was occupied with earthquake reconstruction, the Chinese merchants wasted no time in executing their plans. Two imposing structures on Grant Street, Sing Fat on the southwest corner and Sing Chong on the northwest corner, demonstrate the pseudo-Oriental style with the curved eaves of a pagoda tower. Today's Chinatown skyline was thus a direct response to half a century of the City's hostility.

This new attitude deliberately promoted Chinatown as a tourist mecca, in the hopes that its improved image would help ameliorate the relationship with the community at large. And to some extent, the plan was a success. The rebuilding of Chinatown into an Oriental City was heartily endorsed by the San Francisco Real Estate Board, which passed the following resolution: ". . . whereas . . . the Chinese style of architecture will make it picturesque . . . and attractive to tourists . . . the San Francisco Real Estate Board does hereby recommend to all property owners, to have their buildings re-built with fronts of Oriental and artistic appearance." Architect Clarence R. Ward was requested by leading merchants in San Francisco to set an architectural example. Ward was concerned that the way the current architectural "aberrations" were being built would be a disaster. But Ward's proposal for the Southwest corner of Washington Street and Grant was not executed and the firm Ross & Burgren was credited with setting the "Oriental" style of construction with Sing Fat at the southwest corner and Sing Chong at the northwest corner of Dupont and California.

American architects at the turn of the 20th century were trained in the Beaux Arts tradition; they knew little and cared less about the architecture of Asia. Their exposure to Chinese architecture was limited to images of pagodas and temples with massive curved roofs with eaves curled at corners, forms and expressions already centuries old. Their challenge was to transform these ancient forms into a new Sino-architectural vocabulary using Western methods of construction and local building materials in conformance with local building codes.

The size of the lots and their location were determining factors in the outcome of the design. Corner lots lent themselves to the adaptation of the multi-tiered eaves to simulate the multi-storied pagoda. Since the building code allowed 100% coverage of the lots, the middle lots left only the street façade for design. The ground floor was maximized for storefront usage, leaving minimal room for a front entry to the upper stories. Therefore fire escapes were necessary as secondary exits. These wrought-iron fire escapes were turned into balconies decorated with Chinese design motifs, such as the stylized "double happiness" character. The top-floor balcony was recessed, with the roof extended to create the illusion of the massive roof prevalent in Chinese architecture. Columns, indiscriminately surmounted by capitals, supported the roof, creating an "exotic" appearance. The eclectic use of standard classical building elements—brackets, cornices, parapets, Ionic, Doric, and Corinthian capitals, antefix, and acanthus—combined with an oriental roofline, furthered the exotic image. But only the use of the colors red, yellow, and green was authentically Chinese. Where buildings abutted each other, the contiguous pattern gave the illusion of an "Oriental" streetscape. Waverly Place, with its concentration of buildings, demonstrates this deception best. The illusion created is a masterful design solution, unique and indigenous, for it is neither East nor West but decidedly San Francisco.

Not every property owner and tenant accepted the spirit of transforming post-quake Chinatown into an "Oriental City." Perhaps because of financial considerations, many of the buildings were basic austere brick commercial structures completely without Oriental or Western ornamentation. But the new "Oriental" spirit apparently met with success, not only in the imagery of its physical environment but in the social image of the population, as the *Bulletin*'s "Pacific Progress" issue (May 1, 1909) lauded Chinatown as "one of the most noted places on the American Continent" and apologetically wrote: "we have . . . held up to the public gaze for too long the racial grief that separates the yellow and white people of the earth. . . ."

Such social gains, however, were limited. The passage of the Exclusion Act declared the Chinese could not became citizens, the Alien Land Laws of 1913 and 1923 ensured Chinese could not own property, and local real estate covenants confined the Chinese to Chinatown and restricted labor competition. Denied participation in mainstream America for over four decades, the Chinese embraced the politics of homeland China, while focusing on the domestic affairs of the community and earning the goodwill of San Francisco.

Politics of China in Chinatown

For over half a century, the politics of China profoundly impacted Chinese America. By the end of the 19th century, China under the Manchu rulers

Kang Yu-wei.

(1644-1911) was near collapse, incapable of repelling the onslaught of Western nations and Japan. Kang Yu-wei and Liang Chi-chao advocated saving the backward, archaic dynasty by reforms to bring China into the 20th century and keep pace with the industrial West. Emperor Kang Hsü supported the movement over the objection of his aunt, the Empress Dowager Ts'u Hsi. The Empress Dowager engineered a coup d'état and Kang Hsü was arrested while both Kang Yu-wei and Liang Chi-chao escaped overseas with a price on their heads. In opposition to this reform movement was Dr. Sun Yat-sen, who plotted to overthrow the Dynasty and establish a republic. He also escaped with a price on his head. Both opposing parties sought support for their cause from the overseas Chinese community.

When Ch'en Lan-pin, an envoy who headed

Sun Yat-sen.

the Legation sent by the Chinese government to the U.S., landed in San Francisco in 1878, he witnessed the prevailing anti-Chinese environment in the U.S. and suggested a Chinese consulate be established to oversee the welfare of the Chinese. Titled scholars were sent from China to preside over the *hui kuan*. These officials were, in effect, extensions of the diplomatic services. While these Ching Dynasty representatives were concerned with diffusing the hostilities with the community at large, the two opposing parties of Kung Yu-wei and Sun Yat-sen were actively recruiting sympathizers to overthrow the very government that accorded them protection in the U.S. Each faction had the support of newspapers to propagandize their cause. The future of China was plotted right here in Chinatown.

In the struggle, Sun's revolutionary ideology, to drive out the Manchu rulers and restore China back to the Chinese, prevailed. On October 10, 1911, while Sun Yat-sen was still in the U.S., a rebellion broke out at Wuchan, Hankow, and the Manchu government was overthrown. On November 5, 1911, all of Chinatown came out to celebrate the momentous occasion with a grand parade, followed by a huge banquet. Chinese men cut off their queues, symbolically removing the Manchu's shackles. Fortuitously, the act was also a symbol of Americanization, as the last vestige of Chinese dress was removed. The yellow flag with blue Imperial dragon flew for the last time. Every flagpole in Chinatown flew the flag of the new Republic of China.

But the euphoria was short lived, for the problems of the new Republic had only just begun. Feudal warlords controlled various parts of the country and fought each other for sovereignty. From the East, Japan determined that she should be the power in Asia. After Commodore Matthew Perry opened its doors to Western trade in 1858, Japan took only a short span of less than 50 years to emerge as a military power. She began her aggression, conducting military forays into China. For three decades Chinatown was embroiled in activities to raise funds for the salvation of China.

Following the 1911 Revolution, Dr. Sun consolidated his political activities under the party name Kuomintang (KMT) and strengthened his military forces with the establishment of the Whampoa Military Academy, under a young officer named Chiang Kai Shek. With Sun's death on March 12, 1915, Chiang took command of the KMT and led the fight against Japan. For the next three decades, the overseas Chinese continued to be embroiled in the politics of China and established chapters of the KMT throughout the United States. Since 1915, the KMT headquarters in San Francisco has been at 830-48 Stockton Street. The local press covered the news of the war daily. Orchestrated by the Chinese Six Companies, the Chinese throughout the United States were unified in effort to defeat Japan.

Born American of Chinese Descent

Whether native-born or alien, Chinese Americans were always considered foreigners. As Charles Caldwell Dobie wrote in his 1936 book *San Francisco's Chinatown*, "Here no matter how much they adopt our traditions, they can never hope to enter fully into a birthright." Set apart from Eurocentric America, the first generation of Chinese Americans embraced the politics and culture of the homeland and imparted those values to their offspring, lest their heritage be forgotten. Chinese-language schools were a prominent necessity in the community. This attempt at cultural maintenance began sporadically under the Ching government, but after the 1911 revolution, the *hui kuan* took up the responsibility and established language schools for youths belonging to their association. The Christian missions, recognizing the advantage of enrolling youths into their membership, likewise established Chinese classes.

By 1934, there were 1,708 students, ages six to seventeen, attending ten schools weekdays from 5 p.m. to 8 p.m. after public school and from 9 a.m. to 12 noon on Saturdays. Tuition was $1.00 to $1.50

a month. The degree of success in cultural main-tenance was minimal, but the benefit of "babysit-ting" was universal. Perhaps this contributed to the absence of major juvenile delinquency within the community at the time. Teaching followed the old traditions of China. In the non-missionary schools, teachers admonished and berated the American-born as *mo no* ("no brain") and *jook sing* ("knots of the bamboo"). Corporal punishment was adminis-tered without regard to injury. Today we would con-sider it child abuse.

Although dominated by provincialism within, the American-born generation was not immune to the influences of the country they inhabited. Com-munity life, religion, entertainment, fashion, music, and sports mirrored that of the white middle class. In the Chinese community, the Chinese Young Men's Christian Association, community busi-nesses, and social organizations sponsored sport tournaments. By the 1920s, the Chinese YMCA had become a center for sports. Sporting events in-cluded competition with other YMCAs in the City. These events were about more than winning a game or running a race. They provided opportunities to socialize with people outside of the community.

In the big band era of the 1930s, the music of Benny Goodman, Tommy Dorsey, and Glenn Miller swept the nation. Chinatown likewise was in full swing. On weekends, the gymnasium of the Chinese Young Women's Christian Association and the hall of the Chinese American Citizens Al-liance were jammed with young crowds dancing to the music of the Cathayans or the Chinatown

Mme. Chiang Kai Shek.

Knights. With patriotic fervor, not forgetting the struggle against Japanese aggression in their ancestral homeland, the bands also gave their services to the China War Relief and Rice Bowl, raising funds for war-torn China in the years 1938-1946.

On December 7, 1941, Japan bombed Pearl Harbor! Never in the history of the United States was there such upheaval of the masses as the whole nation mobilized for war. Patriotism bonded people of different colors and backgrounds. Patriotism also blinded us from justice as we branded fellow Americans "the enemy" because they were born of Japanese descent. Under President Franklin D. Roosevelt's Executive Order 8066, people of Japanese ancestry, citizens or not, were herded to internment camps—their businesses abandoned, their properties sold pennies to the dollar. On the other hand, the Chinese were embraced as allies against a common enemy.

No single person did more to change the attitude of America toward the Chinese than the first lady of China, Mme. Chiang Kai Shek, during her goodwill tour of the United States in February 1943, fourteen months after Japan's attack on Pearl Harbor. Christian, educated at Wellesley College, speaking flawless English, she was immediately accepted by America. For six weeks, newspaper headlines and press reports of her grace, charm, and intellect held the nation spellbound. Her welcome to the White House, hosted by America's First Lady Eleanor Roosevelt and President Franklin D. Roosevelt, was unprecedented. Never in the history of America had a Chinese person commanded such influence and authority as she addressed the Senate and the House of Representatives. As she continued her nationwide tour, hundreds of thousands gathered, cheered, and responded with standing ovations, at New York City Hall Plaza, Madison Square Garden, Carnegie Hall, and Boston's Symphony Hall. Mme. Chiang was the model for the thousands of Chinese in the United States. In San Francisco Mme. Chiang's speaking engagement was at the Civic Auditorium, where the Cathay Band was invited to perform. Band member Wilson Wong reflected on that moment with pride: "We (the Chinese) were allowed to play in the Civic Auditorium for the first time ever!" The band opened the ceremony with the national anthems of the two countries, the "Star Spangled Banner" and China's grand march "Qi Lai" or "Arise!"—a symbol of better times to come. In Chinatown, Mme. Chiang spoke to the audience in Mandarin at the

FOR JUSTICE—
For Chinese,
American Friendship
WRITE, WIRE
Your CONGRESSMAN Today
Asking Him To Support The
REPEAL of the CHINESE
EXCLUSION ACT!
Congress Convenes September 13th
Legislation to Repeal   You Can Help Right Now!

Time was right to pressure Congress to repeal the Exclusion Act.

Great China Theatre (now the Great Star) on Jackson Street. With every pause or at the end of every sentence, a thunderous applause brought the house down, despite the fact that most of the audience understood only Cantonese!

World War II and the Civil Rights Movement of the '60s and '70s were the two major historical events that profoundly changed the social milieu of Chinese America. Emerging from decades of exclusion, the Chinese were thrust into mainstream America as comrades in arms. The Exclusion Acts were repealed, allowing a token 105 per year to immigrate, but most importantly, foreign-born Chinese were now eligible to become citizens. Following the war, civil service, private industries, and businesses lowered their barriers toward employment of the Chinese. There was yet one bastion to surmount. In peacetime memories were short, and the spirit of wartime camaraderie was left on the battlefield. We can die together in the same foxhole but we cannot live together in the same neighborhood. It took Civil Rights legislation of the '60s and '70s to open the doors to equal housing with the passage of the California Rumford Fair Housing Act of 1963 and President John F. Kennedy's executive order (1063) to end racial discrimination in housing.

The 1960s were tumultuous times that transformed the Nation. America was divided by the Vietnam War and confused by the counterculture of "hippies" rejecting the values of their middle-class parents and the "establishment," dropping out of society, abandoning social conventions, experimenting with mind-expanding drugs, and advocating sexual freedom with the slogan "make love not war." It was a period of racial, gender, and ethnic awareness. It took protests and riots from the black community against discrimination to prompt the passage of anti-discriminatory laws to end segregation and unfair legislation in housing, employment, and voting.

The Civil Rights Movement had its roots in the 1950s when African Americans dared to challenge segregation in the South, where intimidation by the Ku Klux Klan, murders, lynching, and bombing were still tolerated. Following Rosa Parks's arrest for refusing to give up her seat on the bus to a white person, blacks took action by deliberately sitting in the white section of buses, staging sit-ins at lunch counters, organizing boycotts against white merchants who discriminated against them, and attempting to desegregate the Central High School in Little Rock, Arkansas. But these incidents in the '50s did not as yet raise the consciousness of equal rights in the Chinese community, nor did the Chinese identify this struggle with their own half a century ago. The World War II generation, consisting predominately of illegal "paper sons," dared not protest. Furthermore, the improved relationship with white America, sharing in its postwar posterity, would be jeopardized, and the newly gained acceptance of the Chinese community contrasted starkly with the struggles of the black community. Indeed, some Chinese were ready to wear the mantle of "the model minority" who overcame almost a century of discrimination. The improved relationship led to the Immigration Act of 1965, effective 1968, which eliminated the racial bias of previous acts and placed the Chinese on an equal basis with other nations, with a quota of 20,000 annually.

Following World War II, the War Brides Act of December 28, 1945, and the Fiancée Act of June 26, 1946, wives and fiancées of military veterans were allowed admission to the United States. Between 1948 and 1959, several emergency and temporary laws were passed to admit political refugees and displaced persons seeking asylum. The passage of these acts benefited the Chinese and expanded the population. In addition, President John F. Kennedy signed a presidential directive on May 13, 1962, allowing refugees fleeing from the People's Republic of China to enter the United States. The liberalization of immigration laws increased the population of Chinese America. The affluent, no longer restricted to Chinatowns, were free to move anywhere. Some saw business opportunities outside Chinatown, but those with limited knowledge of a new language and those who were less affluent gravitated to the squalid, overcrowded Chinatowns, breeding grounds for discontent and crime.

The rise of crime plagued Chinatown, as gangs of youths intimidated the Chinese business community, extorting "protection money," smashing windows, eating in restaurants and entering theaters without paying and slashing seats on the way out. Attempting to solve their own problems, a group of well-meaning, U.S.-born teenagers incorporated as the Leway, an abbreviation for Legitimate Way, and appealed to the traditional established organizations of the community but received minimal assistance. Viewing them as delinquents, the police hounded the Leway and the organization was short-lived. China-born youths, moreover, maintained their distance from the Leway and organized as the Wah Ching (Chinese youths), but their demand for assistance from the Chinese community and the community at large was likewise rejected. A number of its members, politicized by the activities of the Black Panthers and influenced by the Cultural Revolution of Red China, regrouped and proclaimed themselves the Red Guards. Emulating the Panthers, they served breakfast to needy children at Portsmouth Square, with Chairman Mao's *Little Red Book* in their pockets. On the other hand, the Panthers had adopted their own slogan, "Power flows out of the barrel of a gun," from Mao's *Little Red Book*. The black Civil Rights Movement spurred political action in the Chinese community. Aided by President Lyndon Johnson's War on Poverty, social workers organized social service programs in the community. Students, energized from participation in the Third World Strike at San Francisco State College and the Yellow Identity Symposium held at the University of California, Berkeley, returned to the community to fight the social injustices and inequalities that plagued Chinatown. From campus rhetoric to community action, college students joined with liberal and radical elements to go on strike against exploitation of women in the garment sweatshops and waiters and busboys in restaurants, and to rally against the demolition of the I-Hotel and the eviction of its low-income tenants.

Today there are numerous social agencies using the political process for federal programs and grants to assist the underprivileged, such as: Chinatown Community Development Center, Chinese for Affirmative Action, Chinese Newcomers Services Center, On Lok Senior Services, Self Help for the Elderly, and Wu Yee Children's Services.

The new generation, rejecting the dominance of the white majority from without and the authority of the old establishment order from within, became a "new voice" in the community. The Civil Rights Era of the '60s and '70s transformed the political landscape of Chinatown forever. In 2011, in the political arena, Edwin Lee—appointed to replace former Mayor Gavin Newsom after his election to Lt. Governor of California—was the first citizen of Chinese descent to become mayor of San Francisco. Across the Bay in Oakland that same year, Jean

Quan became the first Chinese American woman elected mayor of a major American city. Currently, there are three Chinese American members of the San Francisco Board of Supervisors.

Not only has the political landscape changed, the Immigration Act of 1965 has brought a diverse population from Southeast Asia, Hong Kong, Taiwan, and different areas of the People's Republic of China. Chinatown is no longer strictly Cantonese. The newcomers brought with them their cultural baggage, breathing new life in the community. Food products in the marketplace, restaurants, Buddhist temples, herb shops, and acupuncture all reflect the changing face of Chinatown, but the buildings and old institutions remain, to remind us we have been here since the beginning of San Francisco.

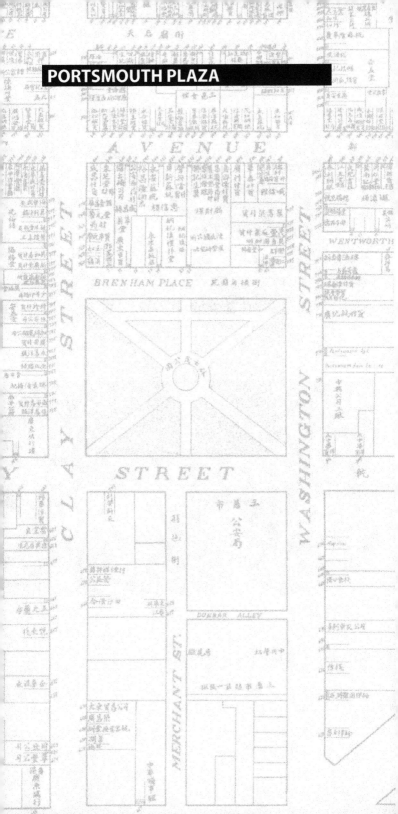

Portsmouth Square ca. 1880s.

Portsmouth Square today.

Once the civic center of San Francisco, Portsmouth Plaza today is the heart and soul of the immigrant Chinese community, used by the young and especially the elderly to escape the drudgery of their often cramped living quarters. When weather permits, women gather to socialize, chat, and play cards, and mothers watch their preschoolers at play, while men hover over players intent on outmaneuvering each other in the Chinese chess game *Jook Kay* ("capture the flag"). Few are aware that they are sitting at the birthplace of San Francisco, where their countrymen were among the multitude of gold seekers celebrating the admission of California to the Union on October 29, 1850. Nor do people realize these Chinese turned the fables of *Gum Saan* (Gold Mountain) into reality.

During the Spanish and Mexican periods of California history, Portsmouth Square was referred to simply as "*la plaza.*" However, when Commodore John B. Montgomery of the U.S.S. *Plymouth* raised the American flag there to claim California during the war with Mexico, the plaza was officially named Portsmouth Square, and the street fronting the Bay was named Montgomery Street. Regardless of its official designation, the early Chinese called it "*Fah Yuen Gok*" ("the park corner"), a name the community still uses today.

The Square was the center for the City's public celebrations and ceremonies. On August 28, 1850, two prominent members of the Chinese community, Norman Assing and A-He, led the Chinese residents to the Square in front of the old Mexican Customs House, where a special public ceremony

The Cable Cars on Clay Street ca. 1880s.

welcomed them to the City. Mayor John Geary, Reverend Albert Williams, and other representatives of the city, presented the "China Boys" (as they called themselves) with Chinese-language religious tracts that had been published in Canton. This event was the extension of the Protestant evangelical movement, the "Second Great Awakening."

For over a century the Square remained a rectangular block sloping down from Walter U. Lum Place (formerly known as "Brenham Place") eastward to Kearny Street, bordered on the east by Clay Street and on the west by Washington Street. In 1960, to accommodate an underground parking garage for this car-congested area, landscape architects Royston, Hanamoto & Mayes redesigned Portsmouth Square into the split-level park you see today.

Clay Street Following Andrew S. Hallidie's successful test-run of the first cable car on August 21,

Kearny Street was called "Ngah Moon Gai" because the Hall of Justice was located there.

1873, horse-drawn cars were replaced with a cable car on Clay Street. Thereafter, the Chinese called Clay Street *"Mo Mah Lie Ch'eh,"* which literally means "no-horse-drawn car." Starting from the top of Leavenworth Street, the line ended at a turntable at the bottom of Clay and Kearny Streets, to send the car back up the hill.

Kearny Street Kearny Street was named for General Stephen Kearny, the first military governor of California, who was ordered by Secretary of State James Buchanan to take possession of California in the war with Mexico. The Chinese referred to it as *Ngah Moon Gai* ("Courthouse Door Street") because it was the site of the Hall of Justice. After the Earthquake, the Hall of Justice housed the Supreme Court, the Traffic Court, and the Police Department, City jail, and morgue. The coming and going of "paddy wagons" and policemen were familiar sights on Kearny Street Although the San Francisco police never wore green uniforms, the

Chinese called policemen *look yee* ("green coat"), a term probably imported from Hong Kong, where it was used to refer to the green-uniformed police. Chinese kids in San Francisco, moreover, used to chant the same ditty, *Dai Tow Look Yee* ("Big-Headed Green Coat"), as the kids in Hong Kong.

Chinese Culture Center
750 Kearny Street

When the Hall of Justice moved out in 1965, Holiday Inn successfully bid to build on the site. Because public funds were involved, the official San Francisco Redevelopment Agency oversaw the project's compliance with government policies, including the Equal Employment Action Program and the Affirmative Action Program. Seizing the opportunity, Chinese community activist organizations such as the Chinatown-North Beach Human Resources Development Center and Chinese for Affirmative Action, along with the San Francisco Human Rights Commission, negotiated construction jobs for Chinese during the building process, and employment at all levels after the hotel's completion.

Likewise, concerned citizens and the Chinese Consolidated Benevolent Association ("Chinese Six Companies"), headed by J.K. Choy, organized and incorporated the Chinese Culture Foundation in 1965. The Foundation negotiated a lease with Holiday Inn at $1.00 a year for a period of 60 years to house a Chinese Culture Center. Initially, the directors of the Foundation consisted of both members of the pro-Taiwan Chinese Six Companies and sympathizers with the People's Republic of China. But conflict developed when the Chinese Six Companies took offense to comments in *Newsweek* by a prominent community member, Joe Yuey, that the Taiwanese government had done nothing in forty years, compared to the progress of the People's Republic of China. Accusing their opponents of at-

Chinese Culture Center.

tempting a political takeover, the Six Companies withdrew from the Foundation on September 22, 1970.

During the dedication of the newly completed Holiday Inn in June 1971, a group of young Asians, the Asian People's Coalition, protested by passing out leaflets condemning the use of public money to build the 27-story Holiday Inn, and the fact that only one floor was reserved for the community. The group argued that instead of building critically needed low-income housing, the City had built 570 luxurious rooms for tourists to gawk at Chinatown. Group members harassed Mayor Alioto and other speakers during the opening ceremony.

In the ensuing decade, just a block away, many more demonstrations would take place in the battle to save the last bastion of Manilatown, the International Hotel ("I-Hotel").

Manilatown and I-Hotel
868 Kearny Street

As with other immigrants from Asia, the coming of Filipinos to America was the result of the United States's efforts to dominate the Pacific. Following the Spanish American War, the United States occupied the Philippines, and Filipinos were classified as United States nationals with unrestricted immigration. After the Philippines Independence Act of 1934, immigration was limited to fifty persons per year.

For over sixty years, the eight blocks on Kearny from Jackson to Sutter were home to Filipino migrant farm workers and merchant marine sailors. The local businesses—such as Bataan Restaurant, Bataan Drugstore, and Bataan Pool Hall—identified the area as Manilatown. Cookie's Bar was the popular hangout for boxers and wrestlers. Old-timers used to tell stories about Lucky Pool Hall, Mike's Barbershop, and Mama and Papa Blanco, who never refused to help a Filipino.

On the east side of Kearny between Jackson and Washington stood the International Hotel (I-Hotel). When the building was condemned, college students, tenants, and Asian American community activists battled eviction of the tenants and demolition of the building. Tenants included nonprofit agencies, such as the Legal Defense Center, an organization founded to counsel young Hong Kong immigrants; Leway (legitimate way), organized in 1967 by former Chinatown street gang members; and the Asian Community Center, which operated

I-Hotel.

Everybody's Bookstore, selling material from the People's Republic of China.

Adding to the area's pre-Civil-Rights-era multicultural mix, Enrico Banducci moved his club, the hungry i, into the basement in the mid-1950s. The nightclub featured such headliners as the Smothers Brothers, Lenny Bruce, the Kingston Trio, and Bill Cosby, all of whom would become famous entertainers. Following the club's closure in 1968, Banducci sold the name to a topless bar that still stands on Broadway in North Beach.

Although the united efforts of activists were unable to prevent demolition of the building, a new building that holds the Filipino History Center on the ground floor and housing units on the upper floors today stands on the corner of Jackson and Kearny Streets as a monument to the I-Hotel's eight-year struggle against real estate development. Sadly, not all of the seniors evicted from the I-Hotel lived long enough to share in the victory and enjoy the benefits of decent housing. Ironically, only ten blocks south at Union Square, at Stockton and Sutter Streets, another monument celebrates Admiral Dewey's 1898 victory in Manila Bay.

Walter U. Lum Place

(formerly Brenham Place)

Brenham Place was named in honor of San Francisco's second and fourth mayor, Charles James Brenham, who had been a riverboat captain on the Mississippi before coming to California. In California, he commanded the *McKim* on the Sacramento River. But on January 14, 1985, the San Francisco Board of Supervisors approved renaming Brenham Place to Walter U. Lum Place, the first local street named in honor of a Chinese American. Walter Uriah Lum (1882-1961) was a native Californian, a leader in the Chinese American Citizen Alliance, and the founder of their newspaper, the *Chinese Times*. He campaigned relentlessly against the discriminatory Chinese exclusion laws. No. 17 Walter U. Lum Place, which housed the Wing Sang Mortuary, the Everybody's Bookstore, the Asian Community Center, and the present headquarters of Chinese for Affirmative Action, has a long history of radical activities.

Walter U. Lum.

Wing Sang Mortuary

17 Walter U. Lum Place

According to Walter U. Lum, upon Sun Yat-sen's arrival to San Francisco in 1904, his luggage was to be forwarded to the Chinese American Citizen Alliance, but was mistakenly delivered to the third floor of the Chinese Consulate, where it was confiscated. Sun found refuge at the Wing Sang Mortuary. The mortuary, a place for the dead, was alive with the clandestine meetings of a group of young Chinese Americans known as the Young China Association, founded in 1909 by Lee Kung Hop with Wong Bok Yu, Jun Oi-won, Wong Wan So, and George Fong. Using the Wing Sang Mortuary—managed by Bok Yu's brother Bak Dun (Frank)—as their headquarters, they met with Sun Yat-sen on his third visit to San Francisco and plotted strategies to enlist more members to support the cause of the Revolution. The group founded the weekly newspaper *Young China* (881-882 Clay Street), with Wong Bok Yu as editor, to propagandize their cause.

Everybody's Bookstore

17 Walter U. Lum Place

No. 17 Walter U. Lum Place was also the home of Everybody's Bookstore and the Asian Community Center. The bookstore was largely founded by members of U.C. Berkeley's Asian American Political Alliance (AAPA), which had been involved with the I-Hotel struggle against tenant eviction.

Wing Sang Mortuary and Everybody's Bookstore.

The Bookstore was an information center for Asian Americans, focused on promoting knowledge of the People's Republic of China (PRC). The store purchased material from Gertrude and Henry Noyes, owners of China Books & Periodicals, Inc., which held the only license issued by the United States Treasury Department to import literature from PRC. Among the Bookstore's initial inventory were one hundred copies of Chairman Mao's *Little Red Book*, which sold out immediately. AAPA disbanded and the core of its membership reorganized as the Asian Community Center, continuing to promote the lofty Communist ideology, "serve the people." In 1980, the building was donated to another up and coming grassroots organization, Chinese for Affirmative Action.

Chinese for Affirmative Action

17 Walter U. Lum Place

In 1969, in keeping with the prevailing mood of the Civil Rights movement, the organization Chinese for Affirmative Action (CAA) was founded to pursue equality for the marginalized minority, using the political process for justice and social change. Milestones in its forty-year history include landmark decisions for bilingual education in the United States Supreme Court case of *Lau v. Nichols*,

Chinese for Affirmative Action.

and the first hiring of Chinese Americans by the San Francisco Police and Fire Departments, which eventually paved the way for the City's first Chinese American police chief, Fred Lau, and the first woman police chief, Heather Fong. A most important breakthrough by CAA was ending the century-old practice by construction unions of barring Chinese from the construction industry.

Chinese Congregational Church
21 Walter U. Lum Place

This five-story building, a version of Gothic revival, was built in 1909 after the '06 Earthquake.

The Reverend William C. Pond, the founder of the mission, grew up in Bangor, Maine, a city steeped in religion. His father was a minister and president of the Bangor Theological Seminary. His mother was the sister of the pastor of the Hammond Street Church in Bangor. The Reverend W.C. Pond, who at six years old had sobbed and cried because he didn't want to become a minister (Pond 1921, 10), ended up devoting a lifetime of ministry to the Chinese in San Francisco. Arriving in San Francisco February 23, 1853, in answer to the urgent call for ministers in California by the American Home Missionary Society, Reverend Pond was charged with raising funds for a new church that came to be known as The Greenwich Street Church. But the parishioners, scammed by ruthless businessmen and dishonest bankers, lost their savings and left the city to seek employment. Reverend Pond spent the next ten years in the Gold Rush town of Downieville in the Sierras. He was then sent to Petaluma for three years and in 1868 he was reassigned to the Third Congregational Church in San Francisco. The surrounding Chinese shoe factories and woolen mills provided the opportunity to conduct a Sunday school for the numerous Chinese employees. An evening school afforded additional opportunity to spread the gospel. In 1868, eight converts declared they were ready to be baptized and become mem-

*Chinese Congrega-
tional Church.*

bers of the church, but the church Standing Committee rejected the idea. After much argument, a disappointed Reverend W.C. Pond resigned.

Following his resignation, thirty followers left the church, rented a small room for a chapel, and named it the Bethany Sunday School. Thus, on February 28, 1873, Reverend W.C. Pond opened what would become the Chinese Congregational Church of today. Jee Gam, who had worked with Reverend Pond, suggested a grandiose plan for headquarters, English classes for Chinese, and a Theological Seminary (Pond 1921, 139). In 1897, the property next to the old firehouse on Brenham Place was purchased and planning began. Architect G.A. Bordwell was hired to draw the plans for the substantial renovation, complete with a chapel, a classroom, family housing, and headquarters for the Congregational Association.

A court interpreter for the City of Oakland, Jee Gam would serve from 1904 to 1910 as the first Chinese minister of the church. He had come to San Francisco with his uncle and worked as a house-boy for The Reverend George Moser. In 1870, Jee Gam joined the Oakland Congregational Church and worked continuously among the Chinese. He became a member of the Bethany Congregational Church, where his wife was baptized in 1884. On September 19, 1895, Jee Gam was ordained at the request of the Congregational Association of Chinese Christians for his twenty-five years of faithful service (Smith 229, note 4).

Jee Gam was invited by the American Missionary Association to attend its annual meeting in 1879. There he pleaded for the importance of establishing a mission to spread gospel in his homeland. He continued his discussions with The Reverend Pond and his vision was fulfilled when Charles R. Hager was ordained as a missionary to China at the Bethany Congregational Church on February 16, 1883. Hong Kong was the chosen seat of his mission (Smith 2005, 93). Reverend Charles R. Hager immediately started a small group in Hong Kong, among whom was a youth named Sun Yat-sen, the future father of the Republic of China! Fortuitously, this was the beginning of Sun Yat-sen's knowledge of the overseas communities in California, where he later launched his attempt to overthrow the Manchu government.

Reverend Jee Gam planned to spend his old age

in China but died while on his way. Reverend W.C. Pond, however, was still active at age 91, not only at the mission, but also in his private life. Church member Mrs. Florence C. Kwan had this story to tell (Kwan 1973, 7). The Reverend Pond came to church with his six-inch-long full beard shaved clean. The rumor among the congregation was that he was courting a middle-aged woman and was about to be married. Months later he appeared with his beard fully grown back. Church members now learned that the family of the women had opposed the marriage.

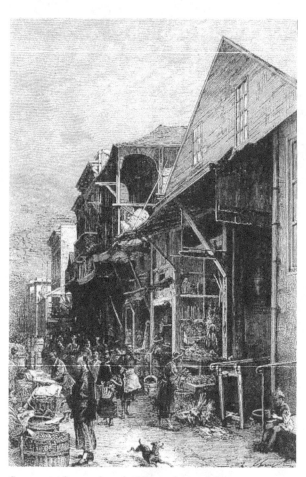

Sacramento Street where the Chinese first settled.

Sacramento Street has been occupied by the Chinese since the days of the Gold Rush. The early arrivals were Cantonese, named after the City of Canton in Guangdong Province. They called themselves "*Tong Yun*" (descendants from the Tang Dynasty, 618-907) from "*Tong Sahn*" (land of Tong). From that time on, the street has been referred to by local Cantonese residents as "*Tong Yun Gai*" ("Street of the Chinese").

Chy Lung Bazaar
674 Sacramento Street

Not all Chinese rushed to the gold fields, nor were they all domestic servants and laundrymen. A few went into mining but most set up as dealers in Chinaware, silk, shawls, and articles of curiosity never before seen by the Gold Rush population. These merchants, who were among the first to emigrate, came mostly from the Sam Yup district of Guangdong.

One of the most notable of these merchants was Chun Lock (1815-1868), who came to California and established Chy Lung on 640 Washington Street in 1850. The *Daily Alta California* described his commercial sagacity and enterprise as being as great as any American or European merchant (DAC 9/1/69). He imported Chinese prefabricated houses and cargoes of Chinese goods, teas, silk, lacquer and porcelain wares, and even opium. The drug that made American merchants millionaires in the China trade now found its way to California for both the Chinese and American markets. Chy Lung was one of only two Chinese businesses at the time that advertised in an American newspaper, the *Daily Alta California*. Chun Lock carried on the business at 676 Sacramento Street until his death in 1868. He was buried in Lone Mountain cemetery, the present site of the University of San Francisco.

His partners continued the business and, after the '06 Earthquake, rebuilt Chy Lung as a four-story building. Contrary to Look Tin Eli's promotion of an "Oriental Chinatown," the building was com-

Chy Lung Bazaar.

pletely devoid of Oriental motifs. Inside, however, the four stories housed a huge stock of porcelain, silk embroidered gowns, bed quilts, jade carvings, and intricately carved rosewood furniture. From its beginnings in the days of the '49ers, Chy Lung was a major art emporium, introducing the public to the fine arts of China.

Chung Sai Yat Po
718 Sacramento Street

This two-story brick-façade building fronting on Sacramento Street from Commercial Street was the home of the *Chung Sai Yat Po*, a Chinese-language newspaper. The present owner chiseled off the Chinese characters, *Chung Sai Yat Po*, engraved above the band at the centerline of the building. On the Sacramento façade above the upper floor windows, you can see a horizontal band with an "Oriental" motif. The head of the windows are accented with heavily glazed terra cotta trim. The Oriental design was kept to a minimum. Continuous remodeling of the storefronts has destroyed the integrity of the building.

The *Chung Sai Yat Po* was published by Dr. Ng Poon Chew (1866–1931), the first Chinese to graduate from the San Francisco Theological Seminary (1892). The newspaper supported the revolutionary cause of Dr. Sun Yat-sen to overthrow the Ching government. Dr. Chew was a well-known Civil Rights activist for the Chinese community, publishing the essay "The Treatment of the Exempt Classes of Chinese in the United States" in 1908, calling attention to the Chinese Exclusion Law as a violation of the treaty between the United States and China.

As a youth, Chew had heard wild stories of California as a land of impenetrable wilderness and the home of cannibals. In one such story, he heard that a group of Chinese was caught but because they were too lean to be good eating, they were held captive in a cave to be fattened up for eating—one

Chung Sai Yat Po.

by one (*San Francisco Examiner* 9/5/1925, p. 10). Nevertheless, when his uncle returned from *Gum Saan* (Gold Mountain) in 1879 and emptied before him eight sacks, each filled with one hundred Mexican dollars, Chew's imagination of adventure and fabulous wealth overcame his fear of being eaten. In 1881, at the age of fifteen, he left for California.

In San Francisco, Ng Poon Chew was derisively nicknamed "*fahn kwei* Chew" ("white man Chew") by relatives and friends because he dared cut off his queue (Hunt 1950, 494). The white public, on the other hand, referred to him as the "Chinese Mark

Twain" because of his oratorical skill and sense of humor. He was invited to speak at the "white only" Commonwealth Club of San Francisco. Rockwell D. Hunt included Ng Poon Chew in his book, *California's Stately Hall of Fame* (1950), as the "Chinese Californian Par Excellence."

The headquarters of *Chung Sai Yat Po* in 1905 were at 804 Sacramento Street. After the 1906 Earthquake, the newspaper moved to Oakland, returning to the City in 1907 at 809 Sacramento Street. In 1915, the newspaper moved one block east to 716 Sacramento Street, where it remained until it suspended operations in 1951. The demise of the newspaper was due to the ever-changing political and social trends of Chinese America. Second- and third-generation Chinese Americans had begun to move outside the confines of Chinatown, and had become less dependent on Chinatown as a cultural center.

Chinese Chamber of Commerce

728-730 Sacramento Street

Chinese merchant guilds were founded early in San Francisco to minimize competition and regulate businesses. In the 19th century, the merchants from the Sam Yup district manipulated trade for the benefit of their own people. The Sze Yup merchants resented this control. The struggle for power led to an ongoing feud that continued for the remainder of the nineteenth century (see Chinese Six Companies).

In 1884, a Sze Yup man was arrested for murder

Chinese Chamber of Commerce.

and the Sam Yup refused to support his defense. In retaliation, the Sze Yup organized a boycott of Sam Yup-owned stores, which lasted for three years, resulting in a number of Sam Yup bankruptcies. Fong Ching, an infamous Sam Yup leader also known as "Little Pete," attempted to break the boycott by terrorizing the Sze Yup. In retaliation, the Sze Yup had him gunned down while he was sitting in a barber's chair at 819 Washington Street on January 23, 1887. Six consul generals were sent from China to mediate the dispute, without success. Finally, in 1899, the Chinese minister Wu Ting-fang took the Sze Yup relatives in China as hostages, which brought an end to the boycott. In 1906 the Chinese Consulate in San Francisco urged the union of the two guilds, resulting in the incorporation of the Chinese Chamber of Commerce.

Today, the Chinese Chamber of Commerce is noted for promoting the annual Chinatown New Year's beauty pageant and inviting organizations from throughout the United States to participate in the grand parade, regardless of color or gender.

Yeong Wo Benevolent Association
746 Sacramento Street

The Yeong Wo Benevolent Association (*hui kuan*) was originally located on the southern slope of Telegraph Hill. The Reverend William Speer described it as "a large frame structure . . . evidently of Chinese architecture . . . with the entry guarded by a pair of lions carved in wood and the portico opening into a courtyard." Established in 1852, it was one of the four original district associations. The Yeong Wo Benevolent Association has been at its present location since 1881.

Yeong Wo Benevolent Association.

According to the engraved date on the parapet of the commercial entrance arch, the building was built in 1928. The Kuomintang (KMT) insignia signified loyalty to Sun Yat-sen's KMT party, which Chinese America embraced at the time the building was built.

The horizontal three-story building contained commercial space on the ground floor and apartments on the upper floors, which at one time housed a Chinese school.

The five-story section used the typical pseudo-Chinese design approach for interior lots, recessing the balcony to create a loggia on the top floor with an Oriental roof overhang.

Nam Kue School

755 Sacramento Street

The Namhoi Benevolent Association, one of the three associations that make up the Sam Yup Benevolent Association, founded the Nam Kue School. The school first opened on March 10, 1920, in a single room on 647 Jackson Street, with thirty-five students. In 1925, because of increasing enrollment, the Namhoi Benevolent Association purchased the site at 755 Sacramento Street and built the present structure.

The school was intended for the children from the three districts of Punyu, Shuntak, and Namhoi of Guangdong Province. Chinese not from these districts could enroll at a higher tuition fee. Chinese schools were established with the intention of keeping young Chinese Americans in touch with Chinese culture, history, and language.

During the Civil Rights Movement of the 1970s, in an attempt to achieve racial equality in education, the San Francisco Board of Education proposed desegregating the public schools by busing children out of their communities into other districts of the city. Parents from the Chinese community were outraged and protested vehemently. When, on July 9, 1971, U.S. District Judge Stanley A. Weigel ordered desegregation by forced busing, Chinese parents, led by the Chinese Six Companies, defied the mandate and opened their own private schools. Four of the local Chinese language schools, including Nam Kue, were used to house classes.

As with all institutions in Chinatown, the Nam

Nam Kue School.

Kue School continued to recognize the Kuomintang (KMT) as the legitimate government of China after its defeat by the People's Republic of China (PRC). With the normalization relation between the United States and PRC, the Nam Kue School was among the few institutions to switch its allegiance. On March 8, 2005 when the school celebrated its 85th anniversary, the KMT flag that flew proudly over the flagpole for eight decades was replaced with the flag of the People's Republic of China.

Chinese Daily Post

809 Sacramento Street

809 Sacramento Street was the former home of the *Chinese Nationalist Daily* (*Kuo Min Yat Bo*). In 1953, the name was changed to the *Chinese Daily Post*.

In the 1920s, the Kuomintang (KMT) was the major political force in Chinese communities. In San Francisco, the KMT was represented by *Young China* (1910-1960) and its daily newspaper at 881-888 Clay Street. The conservative elements of the KMT purged its members associated with Communism. The departing left-wing radicals founded

Chinese Daily Post.

the *Chinese Nationalist Daily* and both parties claimed legitimate representation of the KMT. The friction between the parties was diffused with the outbreak of the Sino-Japanese War in 1937, when the focus turned to opposing Japanese aggression.

Today, the building is the home of *Asian Week*. On display is the exhibit "The Rape of Nanking," documenting atrocities committed by the Japanese during the Sino-Japanese War of 1937.

Chinese Young Men's Christian Association (YMCA)

855 Sacramento Street

Celebrating its 50th anniversary in 1961, the Chinese YMCA traced its official history back to July 11, 1911. However, The Reverend Otis Gibson and The Reverend Ira Condit both wrote of Chinese YMCA activities during the 1870s (Condit 1900, 116) regarding the dispute between the Chinese Christian community and the Chinese Six Companies relating to the purchase of Steamship tickets (Gibson 343). The Six Companies were the "voice" of the Chinese and had quasi-control of all of the Chinese people in America. The Six Companies and the steamship companies reached an agreement whereby any Chinese purchasing tickets to China had to first purchase an exit permit issued by the Six Companies. Members of YMCA refused and in May 1874 sent a memo to the Six Companies releasing themselves from the Companies' "protection" and declaring their right to buy tickets without interference. The shipping companies acquiesced, provided that the passenger could present an "endorsement of character" from one of the missionaries or the stamp of the Chinese YMCA.

When the Chinese branch of the YMCA was established on July 11, 1911, the programs were held in various churches of the community. Expanding membership and activities led to the organization leasing 1028 Stockton Street in 1912, and then 830 Stockton Street in 1915. The present building at 855 Sacramento Street, completed on February 23,

Chinese Young Men's Christian Association (YMCA).

1926, was made possible by six men: John R. Mott, The Reverend Chan Lok Shang, Robert Dollar, John McCallum, Lew Hing, and Richard Perkins.

At the turn of the 20th century an invisible boundary separated the Chinese community from mainstream America, for outside contact was limited to members of certain occupations like food peddlers, laundrymen, and domestic servants. Although the purpose of the "Y" was to promote Christianity, programs such as language, education, and healthcare were also provided to promote assimilation. An employment agency led to working opportunities outside the community, albeit usually as domestic servants.

The appearance of second-generation Chinese in the '20s and '30s made recreation a major priority. The 1925 building provided the first gymnasium and the only swimming pool in Chinatown. The Chinese recreation center with a regulation basketball court, on Mason Street, was not built until 1957. YMCA programs played a major role in the Americanization of young adults and teenagers.

In the design of the 1925 building, the *toukung*, a complicated structural system of timber brackets that supported the roof, was employed by the architect, merely as ornamentation to decorate the entry gate, the entrance to the former boy's and men's lobby, and the outriggers under the eave. A major renovation was completed in 2010, with the addition reflecting a more contemporary architectural style while retaining features of the old as an allusion to the past.

Willie "Woo Woo" Wong Playground

855 Sacramento Street

Until January 1927, the streets or empty lots served as playgrounds for Chinatown's children. On December 4, 1920, the Chinese Chamber of Commerce called on the mayor to build a playground in the community. Though the mayor promised to take the matter into consideration, nothing happened until six years later, when a playground was built on the present site. The playground featured not only Chinatown's first swing sets and slides but also a tennis court, a volleyball court, and a non-regulation-size basketball court. A small field house was built with a pseudo-Chinese design.

The first director of the playground was Oliver Chang, descendant of the Chinese pioneer Yee Atai, who founded the Sze Yup District Association in 1851. Instead of being named after a benefactor of children, the playground remained nameless for over 75 years. In 2009, however, it was named "Willie 'Woo Woo' Wong Playground" after a 5'5" basketball phenomenon of the community who made the University of San Francisco Don's basketball team.

From the time he played in Polytechnic High School during the 1940s to the time coach Pete Newell recruited him to play for the Dons in 1948, "Woo Woo" Wong was acclaimed by sports writers in local newspapers as fantastic, sensational, brilliant—small in stature but large in athletic talent. Traveling with the U.S.F. Dons Varsity in 1949-1950, he was the first Chinese American to play

PROTECT WOO-WOO

*Don Lofgran, left, and Joe McNamee, both 6' 6" tower over 5' 4"
"Woo Woo" Wong.*

in Madison Square Garden and the first to achieve prominence as a collegiate player.

His Chinese name was "Woo" and fans would chant "Woo Woo" every time he scored, so *Examiner* sports writer Bob Brackman nicknamed him "Woo Woo."

Chinese Baptist Church

15 Waverly Place

Early efforts by the Southern Baptist Mission Board to work among the Chinese in San Francisco met with minimal success. Most of the ministers assigned to work with the Chinese community had previously spent time in China and would only work with the Baptist mission for a short period before returning there.

The Reverend John Lewis Shuck was the first such minister to appear in Chinatown. In 1835, he made his first missionary trip to Hong Kong and Canton with his bride Henrietta Hall. After eight years and four sons, Henrietta died, and Reverend Shuck returned home. He remarried and in 1847 returned to China, this time assigned to Shanghai. Tragically his second wife died there and, upon returning to the U.S. in 1854, Reverend Shuck spent a brief period in San Francisco, in an unsuccessful attempt to establish the Chinese Baptist Church. Shortly thereafter, he was sent to Sacramento, where he established a chapel on the corner of 6th and H Streets.

It wasn't until 1870 that the Northern Baptist Mission Board called The Reverend John Francis to restart missionary work among the Chinese in California. Reverend Francis opened a Sunday school using the facilities of the First Baptist Church of San Francisco at 829 Washington Street. Later, Reverend R. H. Graves and Fung Seung Nam came from Canton to replace Reverend Francis. Fung was reputed to be an extremely eloquent and effective

Chinese Baptist Church.

street preacher, attracting a crowd of hundreds on Jackson Street every night. Unfortunately, he died in May 1871, only a year after his arrival. As a tribute, every pastor from Chinatown, and many from outside it, attended his funeral service. In 1874, The Reverend E. I. Simmons, also from Canton, came to San Francisco to replace Reverend Francis, but returned to China after only sixteen months. For the next five years, a small group of Chinatown Christians would continue to meet without a pastor. But missionary activities between China and the Baptist Mission in San Francisco continued. In 1879, Dr. Jess B. Hartwell, who had served twenty years in China, started an evening school in a rented room. Reverend Hartwell had three women, Mrs. J. L. Sanford, Mrs. Mowell, and Miss C.J. White, as assistants but they all went to China as missionaries after only a year.

Nonetheless, under Reverend Hartwell, a Baptist church was finally built in Chinatown in 1888, at the present site on the corner of Sacramento Street and Waverly Place. The building was Romanesque in treatment, employing a half-round arch over double-arched stained-glass windows to dominate both street facades. The present clinker brick building, built after the '06 quake, was originally two stories, with a third floor added in 1937. Only the ground floor was given architectural treatment. A large gothic stained-glass window dominates the Sacramento, Waverly, and west elevations. The composite rose window with four pointed-arch lancets is surrounded by a pointed arch that completes the gothic expression. The second floor is without architectural ornament. When the third floor was added, the architect skillfully replicated the second floor, leaving no clue that the building has been altered. The windows and doors on the clinker brick building are accented with smooth contrasting buff brick to further enhance its architectural appeal.

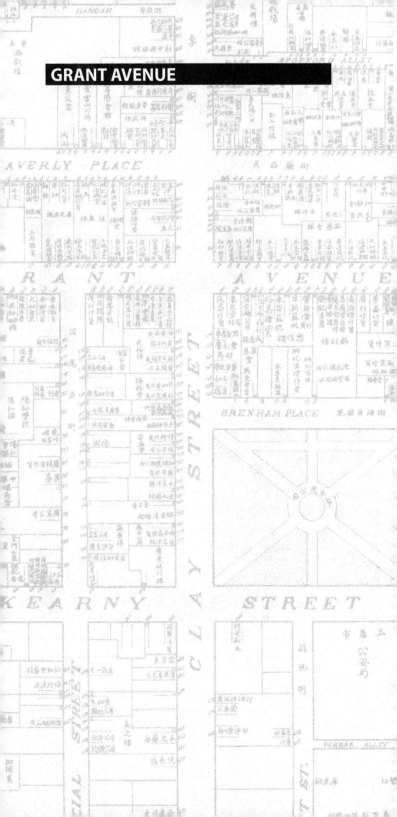

Delivery of live poultry on Grant Avenue between Jackson and Pacific.

Grant Avenue overlays the oldest street in the City. During the Mexican period of California history, the street was labeled "Calle de la Fundacion" on a map sketched by William Antonia Richardson in 1835. On the first official map of San Francisco (as "Yerba Buena") made by Jasper O'Farrell in 1847, Calle de la Fundacion was renamed Dupont Street after Capt. Samuel F. Dupont, United States Naval Officer, Commander of the U.S.S. *Congress*. By the 1870s, the Chinese had moved onto Dupont Street between California and Jackson Streets. Today the Chinese continue to call it "Dupont *Gai*" (street) even though it was renamed Grant Avenue in 1908.

As the Chinese expanded northward in the 1870s, they identified some streets with Chinese names based on the activity of the street, a major incident that occurred, or a prominent place of business. On the north side of Jackson Street between Grant and Stockton Streets—today's Jason Court—was Sullivan Alley, but the Chinese called it *"Gum Gook Hong"* ("Golden Chrysanthemum") after the restaurant on that alley. Old Chinatown Lane was *"Ma Fong Hong"* ("Horse Stable Alley") because the horses and carriages were quartered there. At one time it was called "Cameron Alley," after Donaldina Cameron. On the south side is St. Louis Alley, called by local residents *"Faw Sill Hong"* ("Fire Burning Alley") after a raging fire that occurred on October 20th, 1878.

On Jackson Street between Grant and Kearny, Beckett Street was called *"Bok Wah Dunn Gai"* ("Plain Language John"). According to legend, it was named after a white man called John, an interpreter who spoke Chinese. However, Chief of Police Jesse B. Cook, member of the Chinatown Squad (1880s to 1930s), claimed it was named after the grocery man, who spoke Chinese. On the east side of the street was Wentworth, named *"Duct Wall Gai"* ("Street of Harmony") after the store in that alley. The white public nicknamed it "Fish Alley" because of the stench produced by the processing of dried salted fish in that alley.

These names were used by the Chinese-language Telephone Directory. Other such names are noted throughout the sections of this book.

After the 1906 Earthquake, Grant Avenue developed into three distinct sections. Southern Grant Avenue catered to the tourists, central Grant became the heart of Chinatown, and northern Grant between Pacific and Broadway attracted Italian housewives from adjacent North Beach with the availability of live fish and poultry and Western-style butchered meat.

SOUTHERN GRANT AVENUE

Bush to Sacramento Street

The aspiration of Look Tin Eli for a "veritable fairy palace filled with the choicest treasures of the Orient" began with the two imposing structures on the southwest and southeast corner of Grant and California Streets. After the '06 Earthquake, the two blocks between California and Bush Street became the Oriental Bazaar of Chinatown. Every guidebook included a tour of the two blocks where souvenirs for the tourist and antiques for the serious collector could be found. The lanterns strung across the streets in the '30s were not Chinese, however, but Japanese. The Japanese had become aware not only of the interest in Oriental art but also of the market for tourist trinkets, cheaply made and easily broken. The term "Made in Japan" was synonymous with inferior products, unlike the later reputation for quality of electronics companies such as Sony, Nikon, and Mitsubishi. In 1917, Japanese names such as Daibutsu, K. Yoshizawa Co., Okai Conpany, Nippon Trading, and Madam Butterfly stood out on southern Grant Avenue alongside Chinese firms like Sing Chong, Sing Fat, Canton Bazaar, Wing Sing Lung, and Shanghai Bazaar.

Chinese cocktail bars and lounges—which had begun to appear on Grant in the mid-1920s—began to prosper during 1940s, as San Francisco became a major port for wartime activities. Thousands of servicemen from all over the United States, either stationed in California or in transit, saw for the first time "real" Chinese who played music like Tommy

Dorsey, Glenn Miller, and Benny Goodman, and also listened to Dudley Lee, known as "the Chinese Frank Sinatra," at Andy Wong's Skyroom. At the corner of Grant and Bush was Eddie Pond's Kubla Khan, where Eddie played every Latin American rhythm instrument. Chorus girls dared to expose their legs; Noel Toy, billed as "the Chinese Sally Rand" after the famed fan dancer at the '39 Treasure Island World's Fair, danced with provocative grace, waving her two large feathered fans teasingly to hide her nude body. While escorting her at a recent Chinese Historical Society fundraiser, the present author remarked: "I recognize you!" She quipped: "How can you? I have my clothes on!" These Chinese musicians and dancers were the entrepreneurs of the entertainment world, daring to defy old traditional ways by entering show business.

Sing Chong
601-615 Grant Avenue

Sing Fat
573 Grant Avenue

In the design of the Sing Chong and Sing Fat buildings, architects Ross & Burgren chose the most obvious representation of Chinese architecture, the pagoda. These two corner buildings lent themselves to the adaptation of multi-tiered eaves to emulate the multi-story pagoda. After the completion of the basic structural and functional elements, the four-story steel frame and commercial brick build-

Sing Chong.

ings were topped at the corner with a three-level steel frame pagoda. Whereas the pagoda in China was actually a functional building structure, Ross & Burgren's designs were mere decorative elements added to the roofline. On both buildings, curved canopies simulating Chinese rooflines and placed strategically over window openings enhanced the otherwise austere buildings. The trigram logo on Sing Chong and the dragon trademark of Sing Fat were incised prominently onto the buildings to complete the "Oriental" imagery. At the time of

Sing Fat.

their completion, the buildings were illuminated at night by several thousand incandescent lightbulbs.

Sing Chong, established in 1875, and Sing Fat, established in 1864, were major "Oriental" art stores. Both buildings were designed to accommodate grandiose displays, including large windows on the second floor to display fine porcelain and other works of art. On the ground floors, the innovation of large showroom windows was made possible through the use of steel beams, introduced by the construction of the Eiffel Tower during the 1889 Paris Exposition. The two buildings established the southern end of Grant Avenue (then named Dupont Street) between Sacramento and Bush as the local center for Asian Art. Termed "Oriental bazaars," Sing Chong and Sing Fat offered trinkets and souvenirs for tourists and antiques for serious collectors.

Across the street from the two buildings is St. Mary's Church, built in 1854, a reminder that Chinatown overlays the beginnings of San Francisco. The Sing Fat site itself was where the first Congregational Church was dedicated in 1853.

Old St. Mary's Church

Grant Avenue

Sitting on a foundation of granite imported from China is Old St. Mary's Church, on the southeast corner of Grant Avenue and California Street. The church, founded by Archbishop Joseph Sadoc Alemany, is the only remaining evidence that the Grant Avenue corridor, now Chinatown, was once the domain of mainstream San Francisco. John Sul-

Old St. Mary's Church.

livan, who came to California in 1844, donated the property on which the cathedral was built. Four generations of parishioners, including his children and grandchildren, faithfully attended the church. The sound from the bell of St. Mary's and later the chimes from the clock have echoed through the neighborhood since December 9, 1854. The Chinese called Old St. Mary's "*Dai Chung Low,*" the big bell building.

On the south side across the street from the church were houses of prostitution, openly operated day and night, not by Chinese, but by white women. Such an environment surrounding the church was not acceptable to the congregation. A new St. Mary's Church was completed on Van Ness Avenue on January 11, 1891, and Old St. Mary's was slated for demolition. The Paulist Fathers saved the day and took over the site to do missionary work among down and out elements in the surrounding area. In 1902, missionary work with the Chinese began.

(See Chinese St. Mary's Mission.)

St. Mary's Square

California and Grant Streets

Standing in St. Mary's Square is an imposing stainless steel statue of Dr. Sun Yat-sen designed by Benny Bufano, commissioned by the Chinese Six Companies to commemorate October 10, 1911, the day Dr. Sun's revolutionary party overthrew the Manchu government and established the Republic of China. For almost a century, October 10th, known by the Chinese as "Ten Ten," was a major day of celebration in the community. Banners stretched across Grant Avenue. Organized by the Chinese Six Companies, drum & bugle corps and pupils from every Chinese language school dutifully paraded through the streets. Today the celebration no longer has 100% community support. Members of the Chinese Six Companies are divided; some still embrace the Kuomintang (KMT) Party of

Plaque commemorating Chinese American Veterans of World Wars I and II.

the former Republic of China (now the Taiwanese Government), while others support the People's Republic of China.

Across from the statue of Dr. Sun Yat-sen is a less imposing but more significant monument, with 97 names of Chinese American soldiers of our community, who made the supreme sacrifice in World War I and II. Every year on Veteran's Day, the Cathay Post No. 384 and the VFW Chinatown Post march to the square to honor those who died for us, that they never be forgotten. This commemorative plaque and day of remembrance are more symbolic of Chinese America than Sun Yat-sen's statue and the "Ten Ten" celebration.

CENTRAL GRANT AVENUE

(Sacramento to Jackson Street)

This area marks the beginning of San Francisco (then Yerba Buena) when William Richardson set up his tent on June 25, 1835 (now 823 Grant) and Jacob Leese built his house on the southwest corner of Clay Street on July 4, 1836.

Whereas after the '06 quake, southern Grant developed into a section of Oriental bazaars for tourists, central Grant remained the heart of Chinatown, where businesses were owned and operated by Chinese and for Chinese. In the early 20th century, manufacturing of shoes, boots, and cigars declined while the import and export activities of the *Jop faw poh* (general merchandise stores) increased. Chinatown had begun to make the transition from light manufacturing to import and export activities. Stores hung out their Wells Fargo Express signs daily. Goods imported from China were shipped throughout the numerous Chinese communities in California and across the United States. The sidewalks were blocked with merchandise, and the streets teemed with horses and wagons hauling cargo back and forth to the waterfront. Chinese called the waterfront "*mah ta'ow*" ("horse-front," meaning where horses headed to).

Chinese engaged in the drayage activities were Tom Gunn (later the aviator), his brother Tom Wing, and Frank Dunn (son of the owner of Wing Sang Mortuary), who hauled food across the Bay to Chinese refugees in Oakland. After a year with the Tom brothers, Frank partnered with three oth-

Drayage wagons on Grant Avenue.

ers to form the Canton Express, contracting with the China Mail to carry passengers and baggage. Likewise, Joseph Tape—father of Mamie Tape (see Gordon Lau Elementary School)—had an exclusive contract with Southern Pacific Railroad. Peck Drayage Company and two white-owned drayage companies also operated in Chinatown. The Canton Express was the first to buy a three-ton truck driven by Frank and contracted exclusively with Lew Hing's Cannery to haul fruit and vegetables.

By the beginning of the 1930s, the days of peddling goods with horse-drawn carts clip-clopping over the cobblestone and brick streets of Chinatown had come to an end. The few remaining vendors were from other ethnic populations. With the advent of the automobile, Grant Avenue became a two-way street with parking on both sides. The saying was, when you could drive through Chinatown without a scratch, you were ready to take your driving test. The parked cars, most with out-of-state license plates, attested to Chinatown's popularity as a tourist attraction. At 4:30 p.m., the siren from the Ferry Building signaled the time to head for Chinese school. Kids on the way to school would make a game of seeing who was the quickest to discover a new out-of-state license plate, and, if they had a penny or two, they could stop at one of the corner sidewalk stalls to buy chewing gum.

Sidewalk Stalls

Before the '06 Earthquake, there were sidewalk businesses conducted alongside the buildings at major street intersections. Crude open cabinets with shelves were propped up against the building walls to display the merchandise. These businesses reflected modest enterprises in premium commercial space. After the quake, the buildings were built to accommodate these businesses by recessing the wall about 16 inches deep and 24 feet in length. The shelves in the stalls were packed with an array of merchandise, from edibles like fresh sugar cane, sugar coconuts and melons, varieties of preserved plums, dried ginger, and olives, to dry goods like toilet paper, cigarettes, and cigars of every brand. One-inch-long dried salted water beetles were a typical treat. A favorite with women was "bun long," betel nut wrapped in the betel palm leaf with two-inch-long sticks of sugared coconut, sold two for a nickel. Chewing betel nut is a thousand-year-old tradition throughout Asia. For the kids, the favorite was chewing gum, one cent apiece, packed with a 2"x3" card featuring Remington's paintings of the Wild West. These trading cards provided hours of recreation.

The stalls, formerly at almost every intersection of Grant Avenue, were a distinctive feature in the streetscape of Chinatown. The two remaining stalls along Grant Avenue, at the northwest corners of Clay Street and Washington Street, are mere shadows of their former selves, selling mostly souvenir caps and T-shirts.

At 8:00 p.m. Chinese school was over and the

Sidewalk stall on corner of Clay and Waverly.

streets came alive with children on their way home, chattering in a mixed jargon of English and Chinese, and marching to the "boom boom" cadence of the bass drum of the Salvation Army, whose members were returning to their headquarters on the northeast corner of Sacramento and Grant, after a night of street preaching. The Salvation Army was euphemistically nicknamed the *"Boom Boom Hui"* (association) after the sound of their drums. The establishment of the Salvation Army in Chinatown was consistent with the evangelical movement to "save the Chinamen" with her "Chinese Division . . . to attack China's four hundred millions in their homeland" (McKinley 1986, 50).

Streetlamps
Chinatown, in concert with the City, celebrated the San Francisco's Diamond Jubilee with the installation of the Chinoiserie streetlamps which, along

Chinoiserie streetlamp designed by W. D'arcy Ryan.

with the "Path of Gold" streetlights on Market Street, were designed by W. D'arcy Ryan. Ryan was the Director of Illumination for the 1915 Panama-Pacific Exposition. Around 2005, additional lamps were installed on the side streets off Grant Avenue.

Chinatown Squad

Standing at the corner of Sacramento and Dupont Streets, Inspector Manion, known by the Chinese as "*mow yee*" ("the cat"), might have reminisced with fellow plainclothes detectives about the notorious

The Chinatown Squad.

Tong wars of days past, when the Wongs were at war with the Lees, or the Hop Sing Tong with the Suey Sing Tong. The press credited *"mow yee"* for single-handedly stomping out the Tong wars by forcing the Tongs to sign a peace treaty. The story is somewhat romanticized, as the treaty was written in Chinese, and Manion himself admitted, "no one can stop them, they can only stop themselves." To his credit, however, Manion did much in the Chinatown community, working with Donaldina Cameron to stamp out the traffic in prostitution. Gambling, on the other hand, continued. In the still of the night, from a man standing at a corner, came the chant: *"Su'ong ch'eh fot choy"* ("Get in the car and make your fortune"). Drivers stood ready to taxi clients to gambling houses across the county line in San Mateo.

On June 19, 1954, Lee Dai Ming, editor of the *Chinese World*, pointed out the racial profiling inherent in the continued existence of the Chinatown Squad and called for its dissolution. Although feature writers of local newspaper agreed that the Squad's existence perpetuated past stereotypes of hatchetmen and Tong wars, Chief Michael Gaffey resisted and made no changes. It wasn't until September 14, 1970, that the Chinatown Squad was disbanded. In the era of Civil Rights when the spirit of equality prevailed, Chinatown should not be treated differently from other districts of the City.

Cathay Band

For over fifty years the Cathay Band could be seen on Sundays marching somberly on Grant Avenue, leading a funeral procession to the tune of "Nearer, My God, to Thee." The Band began in 1911 with thirteen boys, ages nine to sixteen, from the Chung Wah Chinese school drum and bugle corps, which petitioned the Chinese Six Companies for help. These thirteen boys were Edward Dong, James Hall, brothers Frank and Thomas Kwan and brothers Thomas, Francis, Herbert, and Frank Lym, Charles Mar, Lee Quong, Andrew Quon Gong, Chang Yoke Liang, and Hugh Liang.

In the prevailing climate of discrimination, Chung Wah asked the Chinese Six Companies to sponsor the Cathay Band, who would become musical goodwill ambassadors to help change public opinion of the Chinese. After one year of practice the band made their debut. Secretary Thomas Kwan wrote: "This first engagement was a great success, not in music . . . but these impressions of the modern Chinese youths was [sic] adequate."

Seventeen years later, in April 1928, the Cathy

Cathay Band.

Band appeared with their newly fashioned Chinese uniforms at the grand opening of the new Los Angeles City Hall. With patriotic fervor and ethnic pride, they played John Philip Sousa's "Stars & Stripes Forever." Band member Chester Look remembered: "The eyes of many nations were upon us, the sons of Hon . . . pride of the Celestial Kingdom. Our last note floating away . . . the thunderous applause . . . was a thrill that neither time nor space can erase!"

Jop Faw Poh (General Merchandise)

After the '06 Earthquake, San Francisco's Chinatown was the export and import center for Chinese commodities for Chinese communities throughout the Nation. Chinese everywhere depended on China for rice, cooking oil, and other food staples. Bundles of rice weighing about fifty pounds came wrapped in rattan mats.

East side of Grant Avenue between Jackson and Pacific.

At the counter, a bookkeeper could be seen tallying up the accounts payable and receivable with his abacus or taking bets on the day and night Chinese lottery called "white pigeon." The casinos of Reno and Las Vegas copied this lottery and called it "Keno," using numbers in lieu of the Chinese characters on the Keno tickets. For almost a century, the policemen of the Chinatown Squad raided and battered down doors with axes to stop the illegal gambling, to no avail. However, when the federal government established the Kefauver Committee in 1950 to investigate narcotic trafficking and organized crime nationwide, Chinatown lotteries stopped abruptly. Congress enacted legislation requiring a federal tax stamp to operate gambling operations. Most of the Chinese lotteries were operated by Chinese with questionable immigration status. Rather than subject themselves to the scrutiny of federal authorities, they chose to close their operations.

A local legend has been woven around the thousand-year-old abacus versus America's then-latest technology, the adding machine. The story goes that a white salesman carried this new bulky invention from store to store, trying to convince Chinese owners to purchase it. One owner said he would buy it if the salesman could demonstrate it to be more efficient than the abacus. The race was on! Of course the outcome of the story is that the salesman walked off defeated, as ethnic one-upmanship must prevail.

Since the purpose of treaties made by the United States with China was for the privilege of trade, Chinese merchants and their families were exempted from the exclusion laws and permitted to immigrate. Chinese circumvented the exclusion laws by claiming merchant status. It was not unusual to find twenty or more members invested in a relatively small *jop faw poh* operation.

It was common practice for stores to provide meals for their employees and makeshift lodging to accommodate single men. In the basement of the stores, a brick stove was built in place with two woks, much like ones in Chinese villages. Instead of using dry branches for fuel, however, gas burners fired up the woks.

Food Facts and Fables

Chinese food was first introduced to our Western frontier during the Gold Rush. For the next 100 years, all Chinese food in America came only from immigrants coming from Guangdong Province. In

Pedi-food carrier on north side of Washington Street, between Grant and Stockton.

fact, until 1961, all the restaurants featured by the Chinese Chamber of Commerce in its New Year publication were Cantonese.

In the madness of the Gold Rush, few prospectors thought to provide service for the burgeoning population. Ever astute, some Chinese found their "gold" in opening restaurants. These Chinese served not only Cantonese food that the '49ers raved about, but also many genuine English dishes with tea and coffee, which were judged "unsurpassed" (Taylor 1850, 117).

The early acceptance of Chinese food was short-lived, however; rumblings of anti-Chinese sentiments beginning in the Mother Lode echoed throughout California for over five decades. Rumors of "meows, bow wows, and rats" (i.e., cats, dogs, and rats) in the larder discouraged even the boldest from setting foot in a Chinese restaurant, save for the occasional banquet welcoming political visitors.

Following the 1906 Earthquake, a new positive image of Chinatown prevailed and guidebooks began to encourage visitors to enjoy a dining experience in Chinatown. That experience was "chop suey," the origin of which was attributed to Chinese envoy Li Hung Chang, who visited the United States in 1897. It was claimed to be his favorite dish. Legends associating chop suey with Li Hung Chang abound, with each generation embellishing the story. It is not a dish found in China but originated in Chinese America. One such legend was, while on his stay in Washington, D.C., late one evening after all restaurants were closed, Chang was hungry for Chinese food. His chef at the hotel hustled up some available ingredients of chicken, pork, celery, onions, and mushrooms, stir-fried it, and served it to Chang. Voilà! He loved it and asked what the dish was called. The chef replied "chop suey," meaning "miscellaneous mixture." Whether the story is fact or fable, the spread of chop suey's popularity across the United States was phenomenal. In San Francisco, huge chop suey signs, two to three stories high with hundreds of incandescent lightbulbs, lit up Chinatown by night and dominated the skyline by day. Chop suey, chow mein, fried rice, and egg foo yung initiated the novice in Chinese cuisine. For the five decades after the '06 quake, chop suey remained synonymous with Chinese food in America. As late as 1972, *San Francisco Chronicle* columnist Herb Caen wrote: "Chinatown is still a mysterious world to most whites . . . who only know how to order . . . chop suey and beetle juice."

Adding to the streetscape of Chinatown was

the pedi-food carrier with a wooden tray on his head, delivering anything from a ten-cent waffle to a complete Chinese dinner to households or establishments in the Chinese quarters. Jackson Café charged 30 cents for a tenderloin steak dinner including coffee, bread, and field potatoes, delivered free. Wearing his "golf" cap to keep his tray from slipping, the carrier trudged from the restaurant onto streets, rain or shine, at all hours of the day and night, into the "wee hours" of the morning. When it rained, a black oilcloth was draped over the tray, fastened down at the corners with clothespins. Empty bowls and dishes were placed outside doorways to be picked up by the carriers. Lost dishes were deducted from their monthly wages, which averaged sixty dollars. With his meager pay, the carrier supported his family and/or his parents and siblings in China. This was not the promise of Gold Mountain he heard in his childhood. No one knows when or how this service began but, like many traditions, it faded with World War II when food was scarce and rationed.

With the more liberal immigration laws following the 1960s, new Chinese immigrants from Hong Kong, Taiwan, and other regions of the Republic of China, as well as Chinese from all parts of Southeast Asia, introduced an infinite variety of Chinese food, which was no longer limited to Cantonese cuisine.

Herb Shops and Herb Doctors

When the Chinese joined the Gold Rush of the '40s, they brought two notable forms of culture baggage with them, worship of the gods and the ancient art of healing. Herb shops existed well into the 20th century, until 1949, when the embargo on goods from Communist China brought an abrupt end to the business. Today, after the normalization of the relationship between the U.S. and China, the use of herbal medicine has begun to thrive once again.

In the frontier west, the Chinese distrusted Western medicine, while non-Chinese sought the "miraculous" cures of herb doctors. One such doctor was Li Po Tai (1817–1893) from Sam Yup who found gold in Gold Mountain not by slaving in the gold fields but by treating over 100 people daily, Chinese and non-Chinese alike. According to legend, his patients included railroads magnates Leland Stanford and Mark Hopkins. As his prowess for healing spread, people came even from the East Coast to seek his "miraculous" cures. Ever an astute businessman, Li Po Tai advertised his medical prowess with much hyperbole in the English-language press. His office on the southwest corner of Washington and Brenham Place was labeled a sanitarium on an 1882 Sanborn Map. (Originally drawn up to assess fire insurance liability, the Sanborn Maps proved a wealth of historical information concerning the development of urban America between 1867 and 1970.)

His fortune wasn't entirely based on healing the sick. He also made money investing in real estate. In December 1870, Charles D. Carter's *Real Estate*

Herb shops came to an abrupt end when the U.S. placed an embargo on products from the People's Republic of China.

Circulars lauded Li Po Tai as the first "Chinaman" on the continent to invest in real estate, making money out of "white fools." Carter predicted: "Between his profits from verdant white patients and real estate investments, the Doctor will be among our millionaires." This prediction was a bit premature. At the time of his death, Li Po Tai's wealth was estimated to be from $100,000 to $300,000 dollars, somewhat short of a million. Li Po Tai passed away on March 20, 1893, leaving a wife, four sons, five daughters, and two grandchildren. His oldest son and his nephew continued his practice in Los Angeles.

The *Chinese World*
736-38 Grant Avenue

The *Chinese World* was originally published in 1891 as the *Mon Hing Bo*, established by Tong King Chong in support of K'ang Yu-wei's movement to establish a constitutional monarchy to reform the Ching government. The text of the newspaper was written by hand, then reproduced by the process of stone lithography. After the '06 quake, the name was changed to *Sai Gai Yat Bo* (the *Chinese World*). Using metal type, five men worked eight hours a day setting 4,000 characters to make one edition, then broke up the type to return the characters to their cases. Each case contained 9,000 characters.

The paper continued to propagandize the reform movement from 1898 to 1911, replete with the political intrigue of K'ang's activities among overseas Chinese, in competition with Sun Yat-sen's movement to overthrow the Ching government. It was Sun's Revolutionary Party that succeeded in 1911. After the Revolution of 1911, most of the *World*'s editorials criticized the corruption of the new government under Chiang Kai Shek's Kuomintang party and his ineptness in repelling the invasion by Japan. With the ascension of the People's Republic of China in 1949, the paper carried news hoping for improved Sino-American relations.

In its early decades, the *Chinese World* focused on China, with little local news coverage of the American-born generation. Due to declining readership, an English section was added on December 1, 1949, in an attempt to attract the English-speak-

The Chinese World.

ing generation. Feature columns included "Chopsticks" by Ken Wong, "H.K.'s Corner" by Henry K. Wong, and "Ed-Lines" by Edward Chew. Subscription rates did not improve. Second- and third-generation Chinese had moved out and no longer were interested in Chinatown. The increasing new immigrant population was of no help. The press stopped and the doors closed in 1969, ending almost seven decades of publication.

Soo Yuen Benevolent Association
806 Clay Street

The Soo Yuen Benevolent Association is a clan association comprised of members with the same surname, commonly known as a "family." For those with less common surnames, several "families" would band together for strength, often using a historical event as the basis for formation. The Soo Yuen Benevolent Association is comprised of three surnames: Louie, Fong, and Kwong.

Before 1919, the brick wall on the Clay Street side of the then-existing building was used for posting announcements, including challenges of rival Tong members and threats of assassination. Hence it became known as the "dead wall."

To remodel the building in 1922, the architects

Soo Yuen Benevolent Association.

Schroepfer and Bolles abandoned the typical post-quake use of eclectic classical elements with Chinese rooflines. Although the building is a corner site, the architects chose not to embellish it with the stereotypical pagoda-style roof. Only a discretely curved fascia can be detected at the corners of the overhang. At night, hundreds of lightbulbs traced the curvilinear arches of the parapet and overhang. Flouting the Chinese architectural forms, the flamboyantly Baroque design enriches the streetscape of Chinatown.

Loong Kong Tien Yee Association

923-32 Grant Avenue

In 1875, Low Fook, Kwant Lok, Chew Show, and Chew Ten signed a deed at 4 Brooklyn Place, on the south side of Sacramento Street between Grant and Stockton Streets (Cowles 1989, 6), and built a temple to consecrate the four heroes who during the period of the Three Kingdoms (220-265 A.D.)

Loong Kong Tien Yee Association.

swore to defend the populace from the tyranny of the ruling warlords. They were Lew Bei, Quan Yu, Jung Fei, and Chew Wan. The stories of their high morals and heroic deeds of justice have been immortalized in *The Romance of the Three Kingdoms* for over one and a half millennia. The descendants of the four heroes with family surnames of Lew (translated by immigration officials as Lau, Liu, Lowe, or Low), Quan (Kwan, Kuan, or Quon), Jung (Chang, Cheung, or Jeung), and Chew (Jew, Ju, Joe, or Chao) banded together to form the "Loong Kong Tien Yee Association," with a worldwide overseas network including San Francisco. This is an example of a clan association formed on the basis of historical events.

The 1906 quake destroyed the original temple. In 1910, a new building was dedicated at 1034 Stockton Street, although in 1925, the Association moved to its present building at 924 Grant Avenue.

Chinese Telephone Exchange

(Bank of Canton)
743 Washington Street

This building was originally the Chinese Telephone Exchange, begun in the aftermath of the 1906 Earthquake and completed in 1909. The appearance of the pagoda-like structure was in keeping with the drive to create an "Oriental City." The front entry columns, supporting a beam without capitals and set on a base, is consistent with Chinese architecture, as compared to classical Western architecture, in which the capital and the column are inseparable.

The first phone in Chinatown was installed at the bilingual newspaper office of *Mon Kee*, owned by Lee Man Teng, who also provided translation

Chinese Telephone Exchange.

Chan Bill, messenger boy, on right.

services for local businesses. Old-timer Chan Bill, at 86 years old, recalled that as a messenger he was paid ten cents to run back and forth to stores to notify subscribers of incoming calls. Later a switchboard was installed with two phone booths, and immediately there were thirty-four subscribers.

In 1902, as subscriptions increased, Pacific Telephone & Telegraph purchased a site on 743 Washington Street and constructed the first and only Chinese Telephone Exchange, with living quarters on the second floor. All the operators were men and had multiple responsibilities, including cooking and cleaning. In keeping with the prevailing practice of hiring women at the switchboards, women operators replaced the men in 1919. By the late 1930s, twenty-four operators handled 2,300 subscribers, with 14,000 calls daily. The women spoke every Cantonese sub-dialect and knew the phone numbers of every store, restaurant, and institution by heart. The operators, speaking Chinese while operating America's latest invention, were a "must-see" novelty for tourists. To this day, old-time Chinese who were born in Chinatown still call the phone "*hom seen*" ("line"), although presumably this usage will disappear with the growth of cellular phones.

Falling victim to progress, the switchboard gave way to automatic dialing and ceased operation in 1948. Twelve years later, in 1960, the building was sold to the Bank of Canton and remodeled. During renovation the exterior wall and wooden entrance doors were replaced entirely with a glass front. Gone with the original doors was the bronze plaque commemorating the site of San Francisco's first newspaper, the *California Star*, published by Sam Brannan, another reminder that Chinatown overlays the beginnings of early San Francisco.

Sam Yup Benevolent Association

831-43 Grant Avenue

Originally known as the "Canton Company," the Sam Yup Benevolent Association, or *hui kuan*, was founded during the Gold Rush era in 1850 by merchants from the Sam Yup district. By 1854, it had begun to call itself Sam Yup Company, which remains its name today. One of the more impor-

Sam Yup Benevolent Association.

tant organizations in Chinatown, the Sam Yup Company worked with other district associations to promote better relations with the community at large and fought against unequal treatment of the Chinese. For example, when the Geary Act of 1892 required that Chinese laborers register with the government, Sam Yup Benevolent Association President Chun Ti Chu acted in concert with other members of the Chinese Consolidated Benevolent Associations of the United States to fight the issue all the way to Supreme Court.

In the 19th century, the Sam Yup Company controlled the import and export businesses of the community. The Sze Yup Company attempted to break this monopoly by boycotting Sam Yup businesses. A major feud between the two groups resulted in the assassination of the Sam Yup leader Fung Ching, known as "Little Pete" (see also Chinese Chamber of Commerce).

The Sam Yup building was remodeled in 1953, at which time the designer applied a pseudo-Chinese canopy onto the face of the top floor above the balcony.

Yan Wo Benevolent Association

945-47 Grant Avenue

This tall, narrow building, built in 1908, follows the typical post-1906 design for interior lots. The building is complete with a storefront on the first floor, a staircase to the upper floors, and the association's club rooms on the top floors. Small curved eaves project over the openings of the second floor, and lights top the rail posts. The Yan Wo Benevolent

Yan Wo Benevolent Association.

Association was established in 1852 as the Sun-On Company and is one of the original four district associations (*hui kuan*) founded during the Gold Rush. Originally, the Yan Wo Benevolent Association was located in Happy Valley (now Second and Market Streets), suggesting the Chinese population in the early decades of the city's history was geographically dispersed.

NORTHERN GRANT AVENUE
Jackson Street to Broadway

The northern end of Jackson Street to Broadway on Dupont (Grant) developed into a busy market-place for Western-style groceries and meat, inter-mingled with old world traditions of live fish and poultry. After the '06 quake, the markets on "Fish Alley" had relocated here. These markets not only served the Chinese but also attracted the Italian housewives from adjacent North Beach who, like the Chinese themselves, demanded hand-selected merchandise, killed and dressed before their eyes. The meat markets also supplied wholesale meat to the Gloria, San Francisco, and Molinari sausage companies. It was politic to hire Italians drivers to deliver the meat to these factories. On delivery days, wooden cages of live ducks and chickens from Peta-luma ranchers lined the street, and butchers could be seen unloading front- and hindquarters of beef onto their shoulders from the trucks of Johnson & Johnson, Allen & Sons, and Moffit from Butcher Town, formerly located at Fairfax and Third Street near Hunters Point. Gow Gong people from Nam-hoi (one of the three districts of Sam Yup *hui kuan*) dominated the meat markets, while Chung Sahn people dominated the fish and poultry markets.

The Mandarin Theatre
1021 Grant Avenue

The Mandarin Theatre—completed June 1924 by architect A.A. Antin—was marveled at by one reporter as "absolutely modern in perfect accord with Chinese ideas of decorative art." Today, it is a shadow of its former self. Since the 1980s, it has been converted into a shopping area occupied by multiple concessions. Current occupants, local residents, and tourists have no clue that here, once upon a time, Cantonese opera played a major role in the entertainment world of Chinatown.

Opera fans would wait until 3 p.m., when the theaters would distribute handbills with photos of their favorite stars promoting the evening's performance. Performances were given every evening from 7 p.m. to 12 p.m. The popularity of Cantonese Opera faded, however, with the decline of the older generations. Adding Chinese movies to the bill did not forestall this decline, and ultimately the Mandarin was sold and converted into business concessions. The Great Star Theatre, formerly the Great China, survived thanks to the Baht Wo Association from Hong Kong, which began to give occasional performances in 1980.

Cantonese opera has a long history in San Francisco, dating back to the Gold Rush. The first performance, presented at the American Theatre in 1852, was not only for the Chinese community but also for white audiences, prominently advertised in the *Alta California* newspaper. While the dialogue was unintelligible to the American audience, the stage props, the costumes of the numerous per-formers, and some very "agile and dexterous ground and lofty tumbling" were considered "well worth seeing." On December 23, 1852, the Tonk Tong Opera Company, under the management of Nor-man Assing, Tong Achik, and Likeon, erected their own imported theater, described by one observer as a "curious looking pagoda."

In the 19th century, a visit to a Chinese theater was on the "must see" list for tourists. However, the novelty began to wear off as the anti-Chinese mood began to escalate. Condescending writers described the music of the orchestra as the sound of a dozen jackasses braying and claimed the singers' screech-ing pierced the ears. Today, thanks to the Baht Wo Association, the popularity of Cantonese opera continues in the community.

The Mandarin Theatre.

City Lights Bookstore
261 Columbus Avenue

City Lights Bookstore, at the edge of North Beach, was the center of 1950s "Beat" culture. Lawrence Ferlinghetti and Peter Martin started the paperback store and named it City Lights after the Charlie Chaplin film. The store became a meeting place for local poets and writers, and the publisher of many of their works. The publication of Allen Ginsberg's *Howl, and Other Poems* (1956) brought national attention when Ferlinghetti and his bookstore manager Shig Murao were arrested for selling obscene and lewd material.

Jack Kerouac was another noted author associated with the literary scene. Adler Place, flanking City Lights on the south side, was renamed Jack Kerouac Alley in his honor.

City Lights Bookstore.

Pacific Avenue

On the 700 block of Pacific Avenue is the Nanking Garage, a reminder that the street was occupied predominately by garages in the 1920s. Two other garages, plus the Blue Bird Cab garage on the south side, were demolished to make way for the first-ever housing project in the community. On the north side were the Nanking and new Tai Ping Garages.

In 1885, a major portion of the southwest corner of Grant and Pacific was notorious for prostitution. Bordering the west side of the property was Sullivan Alley and to its south was Baker's Alley, called "*Mein Bow Hohng*" ("Bread Alley") by the Chinese because a bakery was located there.

At the turn of the 20th century, the New Century Beverage Company stood on 820 Pacific. One of its major products was "Belfast Sparkling Cider," sold only to Chinese communities. It was concocted especially for Chinese consumption during the days of prohibition. Stories abound as to the origin of

An advertsement for Belfast Sparkling Cider.

the "cider" but, according to local legend, during prohibition, the Chinese requested that the company produce a drink with the color of whiskey, to be placed on banquet tables in order to disguise the real product. This story is borne out by Richard Campodonico, grandson of the owner of the beverage company, who remembers his grandfather adding flavoring to seltzer water to produce the drink. (*S.J. Mercury*, 7/19/06). To this day, "Belfast Sparkling Cider" remains popular in Chinese American communities and nowhere else.

JOICE

STOCKTON   STREET

HANGAM

SPOFFORD ALLEY

WAVERLY   PLACE

COLLIER AL.

GRANT   AVENUE

STREET

BRENHAM PLACE

In 1887, the Chinese consulate was opened in the former Pioche residence, on 806 Stockton. M. Pioche was a well-known French businessman with the firm Pioche, Bayengue & Cle. The first Chinese mission was located at the northeast corner of Stockton and Sacramento in 1854. Today, within the western boundary of Stockton Street lies the complex political, social, and cultural milieu that is Chinatown. Organizations reflecting overseas Chinese affairs, like the Chinese Six Companies, the Kong Chow Temple, the Hop Wo district association, the Kuomintang political party, and the Chung Wah Chinese Language School, stand juxtaposed with organizations symbolizing assimilation, like the Chinese American Citizen Alliance, the Chinese Presbyterian Church, the Methodist Episcopalian Church, and the former St. Mary's Church. All played decisive roles in the 19th century and early 20th century Chinatown.

Stockton Street was rezoned in the 1980s as a major shopping corridor, reflecting the merchandising methods of the newer immigrants. The Chinese food markets are heavily concentrated from Washington to Broadway. The myriad of Chinese food differs little from the days of the Gold Rush except for a greater variety. The same food, with its strange looks and odd smells, still elicits strong reactions from tourists.

Chinese Hospital

845 Jackson Street

Much as they did with its churches, protestant missionaries were the driving force behind establishing Chinatown's hospital. Before the hospital existed, terminally ill Chinese were left to die in a place called the "*Tai Ping Fong*" ("Chambers of Tranquility"). The first attempt to establish a hospital for the indigent Chinese in 1888 was met with the usual neighborhood protest. But the refusal of the City

Chinese Hospital, built in 1925.

and County hospitals to admit sick and dying Chinese patients prompted missionaries to renew their efforts to establish a hospital in the community. In 1894, The Reverend Ira M. Condit of the Chinese Presbyterian Church, The Reverend Frederick J. Masters, The Reverend W.C. Pond, and The Reverend Tong Keet Heng attempted to found a hospital, but this time, the project lacked support within the community, as district organizations were feuding among themselves.

It wasn't until 1899 that the *Tai Ping Fong* was closed and the first hospital was opened at 920

Chinese Hospital on 825 Sacramento Street used both Chinese and Western medicine, ca 1900.

Washington Street. The leaders of the organization were Professor John Fryer from the Oriental Department of the University of California, who had spent many years in China; Dr. B.C. Atterbury, who lived in China for twenty years as an independent missionary and established a free dispensary for indigent Chinese in Peking; and Mrs. P.D. Brown, President of the Occidental Board of Foreign Missions. A Dr. Spencer was engaged as resident physician and a Mrs. Spencer as matron.

In the year 1900, a new two-story building was constructed at 828 Sacramento Street. The hospital used both Western and Chinese methods, employing a staff of European doctors and Chinese herb doctors, and featuring a laboratory and a surgery. Ho Hong Yuen, cousin of the Consul General Ho Yow, was director of the hospital, and its chief herbalist was Dr. Tom Wai Tong, who came directly from China. The hospital remained on Sacramento Street until, following the '06 Earthquake, it was rebuilt on 845 Jackson Street. The present building was built in 1925, with a newer building added in 1977. Currently there are plans to redevelop the whole hospital complex.

Chinese American Citizens Alliance
1044 Stockton Street

This five-story building, with a pair of Tuscan columns flanking the stairway entrance, was completed on August 10, 1921. To promote the "American" identity of its occupant, the design of this building was completely devoid of any Oriental motif.

The Chinese American Citizen Alliance (CACA) was founded in 1895 under the name Native Sons of the Golden State (NSGS). It was forced to change its name in 1912 when the Native Sons of the Golden West (NSGW), an organization established in 1875 for white native-born Californians, filed suit against it for having a too similar name.

Chun Dick, Sue Look, Ng Gunn, Li Tai Wing, Leong Sing, Leong Chung, and Lan F. Foy were officers of NSGS, the first Civil Rights organization founded by Chinese Americans. It was a declaration of independence from the old-world organizations that had dominated the affairs of the community. NSGS's primary goal was to "quicken the spirit of American patriotism . . . and to make secure their citizen's rights." It was born out of necessity in an era when the society-at-large was determined to disenfranchise the Chinese.

In 1902, when the Chinese Exclusion Act was up for renewal, Walter U. Lum and Wong Bok Yue protested on behalf of the organization against Senator Cominetti's proposed constitutional amendment to deny children born in America of alien Chinese parents the right to vote and worked to

Chinese American Citizens Alliance.

repeal the Cable Act, which provided that a woman marrying an alien ineligible for citizenship lost her citizenship. As late as 1943, when the Nation, in a more conciliatory spirit, repealed the Chinese Exclusion Acts, the Native Sons of the Golden West continued to lobby for Asiatic Exclusion (*Chronicle* 6/17/43, 5/22/45).

In 1914, the Chinese American Citizens Alliance began to open lodges throughout the United States. In 1924, the organization founded the *Chi-*

nese Times, the first Chinese newspaper published by Chinese Americans, which continued publication until 1988. CACA also fought for equal education, equal recreation facilities (such as the first playground in Chinatown in January 1927), and equal housing for the community.

Chinese Episcopal Methodist Church

1009 Stockton Street

A store at 620 Jackson Street, between two Chinese theaters, was converted into a Methodist Chapel. The storefront window bore the Chinese characters *Foke Yam Tong* (Blessing and Benevolence) (Gibson 1877, 74). The chapel was begun by Mr. H. W. Stowe and had a seating capacity of 75. The walls were decorated with scriptures and the Ten Commandments in Chinese characters. Behind the chapel was a classroom for teaching English.

The first preacher, The Reverend Hu Sing Mi, came from Foo Chow (Fuzhou). Next came Chow Loke Chee, followed by Chan Pak Kwai, and then Chow Loke Chee (Gibson 1877, 82). The Reverend Otis Gibson from the Methodist Mission occasionally preached there, and Chinese Christians volunteered. The Reverend Gibson came to San Francisco in 1868, after spending ten years in Fuzhou, Fujian Province, and immediately began to raise funds to build the Methodist Mission at 916 Washington Street. The building was three stories high with a mansard roof. The ground floor used folding doors to create three classrooms. The second floor likewise had folding doors to create two more classrooms, a living room, and a library. The third floor served as a sanctuary for women rescued from prostitution and as headquarters for the Women's Missionary Society of the Pacific Coast (WMSPC). After the '06 Earthquake, the site was given to the WMSPC to build the Gum Moon residence for women. The

Chinese Episcopal Methodist Church.

new mission was located down the block at the
northwest corner of Washington and Stockton.

In 1876, during the height of the anti-Chinese
movement, The Reverend Gibson gave favorable
testimony on behalf of the Chinese at a Joint Congressional hearing held in San Francisco. As a result, he fell into disfavor with the public and was
hung in effigy in front of Mechanics Pavilion after
Father Buchard from St. Francis Church delivered
his infamous anti-Chinese speech at an anti-Chinese rally.

Later, in the 1930s, Reverend Gibson's granddaughter Eunice Gibson followed in his footsteps
and dedicated her life to working as a public health
nurse at the Chinese Health Center on 1212 Powell
Street. Minnie Fong (sister of Alice Fong Yu) was
the first Chinese public health nurse.

Gordon J. Lau Elementary School

945 Washington Street

The Chinese Primary School was built strictly to keep Chinese from entering schools with white children. In his annual report of 1858, Andrew Moulder, California's first State Superintendent of Schools, warned that "If this attempt to force Africans, Chinese, and Diggers into our white schools is persisted, it must result in the ruin of our schools." Segregated schools for "Negro, Mongolian and Indian children" were prescribed in 1867 by the School Law, which was amended in 1870 to omit the Chinese.

On May 28, 1878, on behalf of the Chinese, attorney B.S. Brooks petitioned the School Board to make provision for a school for Chinese children. This petition was ignored until 1884, when Joseph Tape, a person of Chinese descent, sued the school district and the principal, Jeannie M.A. Hurley, for not admitting his eight-year-old daughter Mamie into Spring Valley Grammar School. The Supreme Court ruled that, as an American citizen, Mamie was entitled to an education and had to be allowed to enter the school. The Board quickly leased a building on the southeast corner of Jackson and Stone to establish the Chinese Primary School, just to keep Mamie from attending Spring Valley. The Chinese Primary School moved to 916 Clay Street but was destroyed during the '06 Earthquake. A temporary building was constructed for the Chinese Primary School at the southwest corner of Joice Alley on Clay Street.

Commodore Stockton School was renamed Gordon Lau Elementary School in 1998.

Following the Earthquake, however, school facilities were overcrowded and white parents complained about the increased presence of Japanese students. In the 1890s, the Japanese had begun to immigrate to San Francisco and their children began to enroll into public schools. In response, on October 11, 1906, Superintendent Roncovieri merely renamed the Chinese Primary School "the Oriental School." As decided in the case *Mamie Tape vs. Hurley*, Japanese pupils would have to attend the

Oriental School on the Southwest corner of Joice and Clay Street.

Oriental School in compliance with Section 1662 of the 1885 School Law, which stated that, when separate schools exist for children of "Mongolian" descent, those students must attend the schools provided for them. Japanese government protests against the hostility toward the Japanese in California and the discrimination against Japanese pupils in segregated schools nearly created an international crisis. President Theodore Roosevelt, mindful not to offend the Japanese government, attempted to coerce California into giving Japanese pupils the right to attend white public schools, threatening to use "all the forces military and civil, of the United States which I may lawfully employ . . . against California" (*S.F. Chronicle* 12/5/1906, p. 6).

The situation was resolved when Roosevelt persuaded the school authorities to rescind its anti-Japanese resolutions. In return he agreed to limit the immigration of Japanese laborers. In 1907, Roosevelt entered into the Gentlemen's Agreement, giving the Japanese Government the right to use its own discretion to limit emigration of Japanese laborers to the United States. The School Board merely reclassified the Japanese as "Malaysian" rather than "Mongolian."

In 1912—the same year a fourteen-year-old white boy was killed by a Chinese person in a racial conflict, near the Oriental School—the school board proposed establishing a new school on the south side of Washington between Stockton and Powell Streets. Bitter neighborhood opposition resulted, with complaints that the location encroached beyond the western boundary of Chinatown. The proposed location of the school close to the Washington Primary School on Mason and Washington Streets further aggravated the racial tensions between white and Chinese schoolboys. But in spite of these objections, the new Oriental School was completed in 1915.

The Chinese American Citizen Alliance, objecting to the overtones of inferiority implied by the term "Oriental," petitioned the School Board to change the name to Harding Primary School. On April 1, 1924, the Board instead elected to rename the school Commodore Stockton School. In 1998, at the request of Civil Rights activists, the Board of Education approved changing the name from Commodore Stockton School to the Gordon J. Lau Elementary School, in honor of Supervisor Lau for his Civil Rights activities during the '60s and '70s protesting poor housing conditions and the lack of employment opportunities in the Chinese community.

Equally important, the school was also the first

to hire a Chinese American school teacher, Alice Fong Yu. While attending San Francisco State Teacher's College, Alice was warned by the president of the college not to go into teaching because she would never be hired. Being realistic, Alice expressed her intent to teach in China, not in the United States. But, to her surprise, on January 18, 1927, she was officially notified of her appointment as teacher at what was then Commodore Stockton School. Her appointment was a response from its newly appointed principal, Anna T. Croughwell, who was in a near-panic at the challenge of handling a school full of jabbering Chinese with whom she could not communicate. She requested a Chinese-speaking teacher not to teach but to serve as a translator in the administrative office, as well as be a clerk, nurse, and parent-teacher liaison. Only much later did Alice actually teach in the classroom. In 1995 the nation's first public Cantonese immersion school, located in the Sunset District of San Francisco, was named after Alice Fong Yu.

Gum Moon Residence
940 Washington Street

The Gum Moon (Golden Gate) Residence was dedicated on January 27, 1912. This was architect Julia Morgan's first attempt to design a building in the Chinese community. Contrary to the prevailing movement to create an "Oriental" City, Morgan used Chinese motifs in her design conservatively, avoiding stereotypical images. The outriggers supporting the roof have only a hint of Chinese design under the eave; a continuous polychrome terra-cotta frieze decorates the building top, with the same terra cotta applied under the entrance vault. Suspended at the entrance is a handsomely designed large copper lantern. Eighteen years later, in the design of the Chinese YWCA, Morgan would display even more confidence in interpreting Chinese art and architectural forms.

The history of the residence dates back to 1868, when The Reverend Otis Gibson established the Methodist Mission at the site (then numbered 916 Washington). The mission did more than preach the gospel. Preceding the much-publicized work of Cameron House, the Methodist Mission also housed orphans and Chinese women rescued from prostitution. Responding to The Reverend Gibson's request, the Women's Missionary Society of the Pacific Coast was organized on October 20, 1870, under the supervision of Mrs. H. C. Cole. By the 1890s, Deaconess Durant and Katherine Mauer continued the work with the cooperation of Donaldina Cameron of the Chinese Presbyterian Mis-

Gum Moon Residence.

sion Home. Katherine Mauer, known as "the angel of Angel Island," was noted for her work among the Chinese detainees there.

After the '06 quake, missionary work continued. Gum Moon was rebuilt as a home for women. The Reverend Gibson had the Methodist Mission built down the block on the northwest corner of Washington and Stockton Street. Today, Gum Moon continues to serve the community by providing a home to non-English-speaking Chinese women, helping them to acclimate.

Chinese Presbyterian Church
925 Stockton Street

When First Presbyterian Church elder Thomas C. Hambly organized a Bible class for the Chinese, Tong A-Chick and Lee Kan, both former students at the Morrison Mission School in Hong Kong, were among the first attendees. Offering classes in English was not sufficient to convert the Chinese, so a Chinese-speaking minister was requested. The Presbyterian Board of Foreign Missions responded by sending The Reverend William Speer, who returned from Canton to work among the Chinese in San Francisco. Four Chinese Christians, A-t'un, A'San, A-teen, and Ho Ch'eong, welcomed him and together they organized the first Chinese mission in America on November 6, 1853, on the northeast corner of Stockton and Sacramento Streets.

When The Reverend Speer first arrived in San Francisco in October 1852, he visited Tong A-Chick at the Young Wo District Association but was unsuccessful in enlisting him as a charter member of the new Chinese mission. However, A-Chick did assist in raising $2,000 from the Chinese community to build the mission.

Reverend Speer published a newspaper called the *Oriental*; Lee Kan was editor of the Chinese section. As resentment toward the Chinese began to grow, the paper staunchly defended them. Reverend Speer retired in 1859, and was succeeded by The Reverend A.W. Loomis, a missionary returning from Ningpo, China, followed in 1870 by The

Chinese Presbyterian Church.

Reverend Ira Condit, who had been a missionary in Canton.

As the white population began to abandon the area near Chinatown, the First Presbyterian Church on Stockton Street was sold to the Board of Foreign Missions and became the new Chinese Presbyterian Mission. The Gothic-style church was destroyed during the '06 quake and one year later the present building was constructed with a porch supported by classically ornamented columns with ionic capitals. The building has since been remodeled, preserving the integrity of the façade.

Hop Wo Benevolent Association
913 Stockton Street

The Hop Wo Benevolent Association is one of the original six associations that comprised the Chinese Six Companies. It was founded in 1862 when it separated from the original Sze Yup Co., founded in 1851. In 1881, Hop Wo was located at 673 Clay Street, with a notable temple. The present building, constructed after the 1906 Earthquake, may have had an "Oriental" style parapet that has since been removed.

Hop Wo Benevolent Association.

St. Mary's Chinese Mission
930 Stockton Street

This building was the St. Mary's Chinese Mission until in 1998, when it was sold. As of this writing, a new building is being completed at Kearny and Jackson Streets.

In the 19th century, the Chinese and the Irish were the two largest foreign-born groups in San Francisco. The Irish were predominantly Catholic; unfortunately, racial intolerance permeated even the highest ranks of the Catholic clergy. Economic competition kept the two groups even further apart. In the 1870s, when the Irish began to demand higher wages, the Chinese were induced to go East to replace them.

Anti-Chinese issues in the West often translated to Irish vs. Chinese, Catholic vs. Protestant. At the height of anti-Chinese activities, during the 1876 "Joint Congressional" hearings, Father Bouchard in San Francisco gave his inflammatory speech: "Chinaman or white man, which?" The Reverend Otis Gibson of the Chinese Baptist Mission responded on behalf of the Chinese and was hung in effigy during an anti-Chinese rally. The Catholic Church not only failed to transcend racism, but also fanned its flames.

In 1883, the more conciliatory Father Alemany requested authority from Rome to start a mission for the Chinese in San Francisco. Father Antonucci—who had spent six years in China, spoke Mandarin not Cantonese, and barely spoke English—was charged with the responsibility. J.O. Donoghue and

St. Mary's Chinese Mission.

a Chinese Catholic named Andreas Ma assisted him. On March 29, 1883, the *San Francisco Daily Morning Call* described the new mission as a little cottage established on the "north side of Clay Street between Stockton and Mason Street with terraces and steps leading down to a paved court opening on Clay Street. . . . " Immediately there was an attendance of fifty Chinese. But what happened thereafter hasn't been recorded.

In 1894, the Paulist Fathers took over the old St. Mary's Church on Dupont and California Streets. A Chinese mission was started in the basement of the church in 1903 under the leadership of Father Henry I. Stark. The Mission gained its own home when an Irish Catholic layman, Mr. Gleason, donated a house on Clay Street above Stockton. But it lasted only a few years before being destroyed by the '06 quake. Thereafter the Mission moved from place to place until Mrs. Bertha Welch financed a building for a permanent Catholic Chinese School and Social Center on the northwest corner of Clay and Stockton Streets. Mrs. Welch was a laywoman who had worked with Mother St. Ida, who started a kindergarten and English classes for Chinese mothers at Old St. Mary's Church. Both Mother St. Ida and another assistant, Mother St. Rosa, were China-born Eurasian nuns. Father Charles E. Bradley, who was director at the time (1910-1926), did not speak Chinese but he nevertheless listened to confessions. The problem was resolved when in 1920 a native Chinese Catechist, Mr. Anthony Chan, was brought from Canton. The word of God could now be heard in Chinese. To make up for his deficiency, Father Bradley went to Hong Kong to study Cantonese.

For some seven decades, the Mission provided education, health, employment, housing, and recreation to the community. Through its recreation programs, the Mission in the 1940s produced such local stars as Helen Wong in tennis, and 5'5" tall Willie "Woo Woo" Wong, who played on the University of San Francisco basketball team. The Chinese playground on Sacramento Street is named in Willie Wong's honor. As early as 1930, the Mission had its first young men's drum corps and in 1940, an all-girls St. Mary's drum corps made its debut. For seven decades, the girls' drum corps competed in their shimmering silk Chinese uniforms to the cadence of the "Bells of St. Mary's" and brought home trophy after trophy. Alas, in our changing social environment, the original thirty members had decreased to fifteen by the time Senator Feinstein sent them to represent San Francisco by performing at the 2010 World's Fair in its sister city, Shanghai.

The Chinese YWCA
(The Chinese Historical Society of America)
965 Clay Street

YWCA Residence Club
940 Powell Street

The history of the Young Women's Christian Association (YWCA) and the YWCA Residence
Club doesn't simply concern architecture but rather
reveals the social realities of the time. The YWCA
was a nationwide progressive women's movement—
ahead of its time in the promotion of women's
welfare through Christian fellowship—and was
conscious that the issue of racial segregation needed
to be resolved if the Association were to represent a
true cross-section of all women.

Julia Morgan designed the two "Y" facilities
concurrently in the early 1930s. The fire marshal
had condemned the prior Women's Residence Club
as unsafe; meanwhile the Chinese Women's "Y" at
897 Sacramento Street had outgrown its space and
needed a new home. Although it was considered
too close to Chinatown, the proposed site on Powell
and Clay Streets ultimately was selected. When the
Chinese "Y" Committee of Management requested
the planning include quarters for Chinese women
in the Residence Club, meetings of the Residence
Committee were held to consider whether Chinese
women should be housed with American women.
In one of many proposed solutions, Julia Morgan
offered to design separate entrances, one for Chinese and one for American women. The Residential

Committee finally resolved "not to have any connection" between the two housing facilities. Even within these Christian organizations, the deeply rooted belief in the superiority of whites over people of color failed to be transcended.

Julia Morgan (1872-1957) belongs to that pioneering first generation of women architects, working at the time when men still clung to the notion that women should stay at home and have babies. It was her association with such women as Phoebe Hearst and her college roommate Grace Fisher Richards (who became the Executive Director of the Oakland YWCA) that led to Morgan's being chosen as architect for the YWCAs in the Western United States, and subsequently as the designer of the Residence Club and the Chinese YWCA Center. Morgan became an inspiration for women of her generation, a role model who transcended the domestic role and raised consciousness of women's equality. She stood tall among such architectural giants as Bernard Maybeck, Arthur J. Brown, and John Galen Howard.

Because of the intense research needed to design the Chinese YWCA on Clay Street, Morgan came to appreciate Chinese architecture and avoided the stereotypical approaches of earlier trendsetting architects of Chinatown after the 1906 Earthquake. She didn't adopt the multi-tier pressed, tin pagodas and imitation curled eaves. In reference to the design fees for the Chinese YWCA and Japanese YWCA, Morgan during a committee meeting said: "You can't afford to pay for it; it has required so much research, I would like to give it as a tribute

The former Chinese YWCA, now the Chinese Historical Society of America.

to the contributions of those two countries to architecture." The exterior treatment of the Residence Club and the Chinese YWCA reflected Morgan's genius at blending the architectural characteristics of two divergent cultures.

Mrs. P. D. Browne founded the YWCAs in San Francisco and Oakland, as well as Montreal, Canada. Her activities in the Chinese community began in 1894, when she founded the Presbyterian Mission Home for girls (a.k.a. Cameron House), and in 1916 she helped organize the Chinese YWCA. This was done in cooperation with other missionary workers in Chinatown, such as Donaldina Cameron. Aiding the mission were members of the Chinese Advisory Committee, including Mrs. Ng Poon Chew, wife of the Chinese Presbyterian Church minister who founded the *Chung Sai Yat Bo*, Mrs. Theodore Chow from the Methodist Episcopal Chinese Church, and Mrs. H. Y. (Charlotte) Chang. A person who embodied the spirit of the

The YWCA Residence Club.

YWCA was Emily Lee Fong. She spearheaded the fund drive for the new building in 1932. Her commitment to the welfare of Chinese women and to the community spanned two world wars.

Thirty years later, in 1952, integration was finally achieved when the Central Committee of Management declared, "the way to learn to live together is to live together" and during the institution's 75th anniversary in 1953, the Executive Director, Mary Buchtel, reported the end of segregated housing.

The doors of the Residence Club were opened to Chinese and to African Americans. In 1980 the Residence Club was converted to housing for seniors, and in 1996 the Chinese YWCA was sold to the Chinese Historical Society of America.

The Chinese Historical Society of America (CHSA) was founded in 1962 at a time when the society-at-large had yet to acknowledge the Chinese of America as an integral part of America history. One of the goals set forth in its constitution was: "To promote the contribution that the Chinese living in this country have made to their adopted land, the United States of America." The museum features stories never told in the annals of the Nation. Visitors to the museum are generally impressed and amazed at the information they were never told by their history books.

At first, meetings were held in different homes until 1966, when the Shoong Foundation donated a small building at 17 Adler (now Kerouac Place) for a museum. The building was sold and CHSA moved into the basement at 650 Commerical Street. The physical environment was poor and CHSA sought a new location. Joe Ling, owner of the Gum Sahn Restaurant on 644 Broadway, graciously offered CHSA a place on the fourth floor of the building rent-free. Meanwhile, however, the Chinese YWCA was up for sale. Supervisor Tom Hsieh came to the rescue and under the administration of Mayor Willie Brown, the City funded the purchase in 1996.

After renovation was completed in 2001, CHSA finally had a permanent home.

Donaldina Cameron House

920 Sacramento Street (S.F. Landmark #44)

Cameron House began in 1874 as a refuge for Chinese girls. In the Gold Rush era, men and women of all professions and occupations—doctors, lawyers, merchants, tradesmen, carpenters, and cooks—coexisted with gamblers, thieves, and harlots. A large proportion of the very few females were "of loose character." In the Chinese quarters, the women were fewer still.

Writers on the history of San Francisco never failed to exaggerate the evils and sins of Chinatown, focusing on how Chinese women were imported, owned, and bartered in the notorious prostitution traffic. The 1885 Municipal Report documented 66 Chinese houses of prostitution, and 32 white ones, within Chinatown.

In 1874 a group of Presbyterian women, Mrs. P.D. Brown, Miss Eleanor Olney, Miss Margaret Culbertson, and Mrs. Ira C. Condit organized to rescue Chinese girls caught in prostitution. A home on Joice Alley rented to house the girls quickly grew overcrowded. In 1877, the building on 933 Sacramento Street was purchased and organized as the Women's Occidental Board of Foreign Missions, with Margaret Culbertson as director. In 1893, a new building known as Culbertson Hall was erected on 920 Sacramento Street.

The brick building was capped by a gabled roof with a domed turret at the southeast corner. Heavy windowsills and lintels accented the brick surfaces. Romanesque revival details accented the main floor

Culbertson Hall.

windows. After the '06 earthquake, an unpreten-
tious three-story red clinker brick building replaced
the Romanesque structure. The cornerstone for
the new building was laid in August 1907, and in
March 1908, the mission resumed its most needed
activities, rescuing girls from prostitution and providing a home for women in distress.

In 1895, twenty-five-year-old Donaldina Cameron arrived to assist Miss Culbertson. Donaldina
intended to stay for a year but that year grew into
four decades of charitable work, with the help of the
Chinatown police squad. During the years when
Sgt. John Manion was in charge, from 1921 until
his retirement in 1949, the prostitution traffic diminished. In 1934, Donadina retired and in 1942,
the building was dedicated in her honor as Donaldina Cameron House.

By the 1930s, the need for a home for rescued
women was no longer as acute, but still necessary.
To the disappointment of the women still working
and living there, the premise was leased to Hip Wo,
a Chinese-language school sponsored by a union of

Donaldina Cameron House.

the three Chinese churches: Congregational, Presbyterian, and Methodist. The education of children
to maintain their Chinese culture under a Christian
environment was deemed a higher priority. But the
work started by Margaret Culbertson and Donaldina Cameron was continued at 144 Wetmore Street
by Lorna Logan, Tien Wu, May Wong, and others
who had worked closely alongside Miss Cameron.

In 1946, the 920 Sacramento Street building
was returned to the Board of National Missions for
the purpose of starting programs conceived as vi-
tally needed for the youths of Chinatown. The staff
that had been carrying on the social work program
at 144 Wetmore moved back in. Cameron House
continues to address the needs of a society in con-
stant change. Services are provided for youths, from
both within and outside the community. Counsel-
ing is offered for cancer patients and adults with
domestic problems, and services for immigrants
with difficulty acclimating are also provided. Since
1946, three generations have benefited from the
programs for youths, a testament to the invaluable
service of Cameron House.

Chinese Central High School (a.k.a. Victory Hall)

827 Stockton Street

The Chinese Central High School (*Chung Wah*) originally began in 1887 as the *Dai Ching Shu Yuen* (Great Ching School), a primary school sponsored by the Chinese Consolidated Benevolent Association (CCBA). The operation of the school was disrupted by the 1906 quake but was able to resume afterward, when the Ching Government sent educational commissioner Liang Qinggui to North America to indoctrinate Chinese youths in Chinese culture. Liang subsequently established schools in major Chinese communities.

In San Francisco, the Dai Ching school resumed operating in the new CCBA building, built with earthquake relief funds from the Ching Government, on 834 Stockton Street.

On December 15, 1927, the Dai Ching School moved into the building purchased by CCBC at

Central High School.

827 Stockton Street, and the name was changed to *Chung Wah* (Chinese Central High). Following World War II, the school was remodeled and renamed Victory Hall. However, the Chung Wah alumni lobbied to restore name back to the Chung Wah School. The Chinese characters Chung Wah School were then placed on the face of the building but, because of linguistic habit, the term "Victory Hall" remains in usage.

Chinese Consolidation Benevolent Association (a.k.a. Chinese Six Companies)
834 Stockton Street

Since the arrival of the Chinese in San Francisco in the early 1850s, immigrants from Guangdong Province sharing geographic origins and speaking the same dialect organized themselves into district associations known as *hui kuan*. The first four *hui kuan* were: Sam Yup in 1851, Sze Yup in 1851, Young Wo in 1852, and Sun On in 1852. In 1853, a group separated from the Sze Yup and formed the Ning Yung Association. A further split occurred in the 1860s, when the Sze Yup was divided into two groups, the Hop Wo and the Kong Chow.

The *hui kuan* functioned as a cultural shock absorber for newly arrived immigrants, providing necessities such as medical care, food, and temporary lodging. Unfortunately, the society at large saw the associations as importers of coolie labor and slave girls and as controllers of gambling and opium traffic. Because the Chinese immigrants faced hostilities from anti-Chinese forces and had no Consular representative, the *hui kuan* found it necessary to band together as the Chinese Six Companies to collectively fight against both legal and extralegal discrimination. As such they wrote letters of protests against anti-Chinese mass meetings and riots to civic and state officials, including a memorandum in 1897 "To His Excellency U.S. Grant," rebutting anti-Chinese charges.

It wasn't until September 26, 1878, that the first

Chinese Consolidation Benevolent Association (a.k.a. Chinese Six Companies).

Chinese Legation was established in Washington, D.C., with the appointment of Chan Lan Pin and Yung Wing as envoys, followed by the appointment of Chen Shu Tung as Consul General in San Francisco on November 8, 1878. Attorney Frederick A. Bee in San Francisco was then appointed as consul to the Chinese Empire. It then became the practice to bring members of China's gentry-scholar class with imperial degrees to San Francisco to be directors of the *hui kuan*. These scholars were also assigned to assist in consular duties. The Chinese Consul, on the other hand, was an ex-officio member of the Chinese Six Companies. Their headquarters were originally on 917 Clay Street, before they moved into the Pioche Mansion at 806 Stockton Street in 1887.

On December 10, 1882, with the recommendation of the Chinese Consul General in San Francisco, the Six Companies were consolidated as one organization. Branches were established throughout North America in cities with major Chinese populations, with active participation of titled Chinese officials. The organization was not legally incorporated as the Chinese Consolidated Benevolent Association, USA (CCBA-USA) until 1901. Acknowledged as the "voice" of the Chinese American population, CCBA-USA continued to exercise a strong influence on the affairs of all the Chinese communities in the United States until the 1950s.

Whenever a nonprofit organization such as the YMCA or the YWCA went fundraising in the community, it would seek approval from the CCBA; thereafter members of the CCBA would accompany the organization's members, going from store to store in Chinatown to solicit donations from merchants.

In recent years, the sphere of influence of the CCBA within Chinatown has diminished. Before 1949, emigrants to Chinatown were predominately Cantonese from Guangdong. Since 1965, liberal immigration laws have brought a diverse Chinese population from all over Southeast China, as well as from Taiwan, who are no longer restricted to settling in Chinatown.

Shortly after the earthquake, the CCBA was rebuilt at 738 Commercial Street. However, because of the squalid Commercial Street environment, the headquarters were relocated to the present Stockton Street location. The original building did not have a pronounced Chinese architectural presence. However, in the remodeling of the building in 1950s, a strong ethnic statement was made with a typical classic Chinese entrance gate guarded by a pair of "Foo Dogs."

On top of the building the flag of the Kuomintang, declaring allegiance to the Taiwan government (Republic of China), flies alongside the Stars and Stripes.

Kong Chow Benevolent Association
865 Stockton Street

This is a contemporary building using imported Chinese tile to convey its ethnicity. The Kong Chow Benevolent Association is one of the district associations that together form the Chinese Six Companies. The Kong Chow Temple is on the building's top floor, having relocated in 1977 from 520 Pine Street. The Kong Chow and the Tien Hou on Waverly Place are the two oldest Chinese temples in San Francisco, dating back to the days of the Gold Rush.

In 1853, G. Ah Thai (a.k.a. G. Athei, Yee Dy, Ah Tye) held title to the Pine Street building where

Kong Chow Benevolent Association.

Kong Chow Benevolent Association before the '06 Earthquake on Pine Street

Kong Chow Benevolent Association on Pine Street after the '06 Earthquake

the Sze Yup Co. was located. In the 1860s, the Sze Yup Company split into two organizations, the Kong Chow and Ning Yung Company. The Ning Yung moved to 517 Broadway. The Kong Chow Company retained the Pine Street site for over one hundred years, until it was sold in 1969.

Charlotte Ah Tye Chang was the granddaughter of G. Ah Thai and also the mother of Oliver Chang, the first playground director of Chinese descent in San Francisco, who directed the first Chinese playground in Chinatown. In 1969, at the age of 96, Charlotte attempted to save the building from demolition by having it declared a city landmark, with the support of Inter-Collegiate Students for Social Action at the University of California, Berkeley. This was the first attempt by a community activist to save a Chinatown landmark, but unfortunately it didn't succeed. Before demolition, however, members saved all the temple's paraphernalia, including the horizontal plaque with the calligraphy executed by Wu Ting Fang, minister of the Chinese Legation in Washington, D.C., for reinstallation in their new building.

(See Ning Yung Benevolent Association and Chinese Benevolent Association of America.)

Kuomintang (KMT)

830-48 Stockton Street

Following the 1911 Revolution, Dr. Sun Yat-sen consolidated his political activities under the party name Kuomintang (KMT) and strengthened his military forces with the establishment of the Whampoa Military Academy, under a young officer named Chiang Kai Shek. With Sun's death on March 12, 1915, Chiang took command of the KMT and led the fight against Japan. For the next three decades, the overseas Chinese continued to be embroiled in the politics of China and established chapters of the KMT throughout the United States. Since 1915, the KMT headquarters in San Francisco have been at 830-48 Stockton Street. The local Chinese newspapers covered the war daily. Orchestrated by the Chinese Six Companies, the Chinese throughout the United States were unified in the effort to defeat Japan.

Kuomintang (KMT) Building.

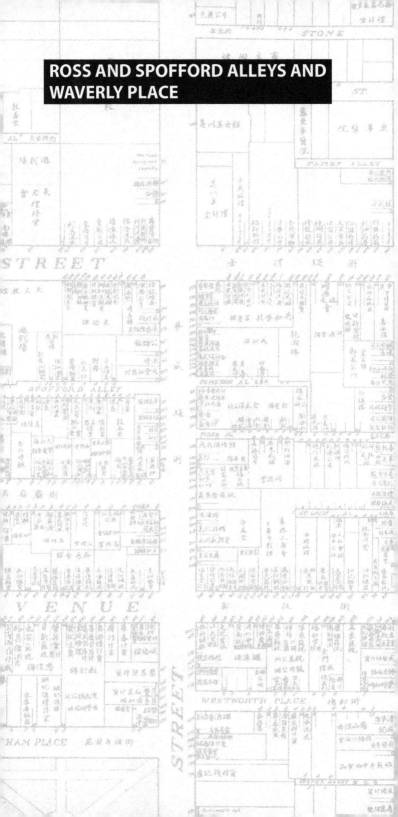

ROSS AND SPOFFORD ALLEYS AND WAVERLY PLACE

Waverly Place was originally known as Pike Street. Since the 1880s, local residents called it "*Tien Hou Mew Guy*" after the Tien Hou Temple located there. In the 1890s, the street was also home to the Kwan Kung Temple of the Ning Yung district association. On the opposite side of the street (22 Waverly) sat the *Sing Wong Mew* (Temple of the City God), while the *Tung Wah Mew* (Temple of the Fire God) was at 35 Waverly.

Westerners have often referred to Chinese temples as "Joss Houses" although the Chinese word for temple (in Cantonese) is actually *Mew*. The word *joss* is a corruption of the Portuguese word *Dios* for God, stemming from the time of Portugal's colonization of Macau in 1557 (Hunter 1965, 61).

The street was also known as "*Ho Bu'un Guy*" or "Fifteen Cent Street," because of the barber shops providing tonsorial services for the price of fifteen cents.

On Waverly Place there is a unique concentration of buildings that represent the different types of traditional Chinese organizations. Architecturally the contiguous line of buildings combining classical motifs with Chinese elements and color created a Chinese streetscape neither East nor West but rather indigenously San Francisco.

As early as the 1880s, Spofford Alley has been known to Chinese residents as "*Sun Leuih Sung Hohng*" ("New Spanish Alley") and Ross Alley (formerly Stout) was known as "*Ga'ow Leuih Sung Hohng*" ("Old Spanish Alley") because they were frequented by Hispanics for gambling, prostitution, and opium.

In the 1870s, when Chinatown dominated the sewing industry, the sewing machine operators were all men. In the 1920s, women began to outnumber male operators and, by 1939, after the onset of World War II, women had entirely replaced male workers. When immigration laws became more liberal, an increasing number of women began to appear in the workforce. Trapped by linguistic and cultural barriers, many women had little choice but to work in sewing factories. Long hours, low wages, and substandard working conditions earned the industry the label "sweatshops." In 1969, wages were from thirty-five cents to fifty cents an hour, while the work hours were seventy hours per week. From the 1950s until the 1980s, the humming of sewing machines could be heard along Spofford and Ross Alleys.

The only fortune cookie factory remaining in the community is in Ross Alley. The fortune cookie became a favorite with tourists shortly before World War II, just as restaurants became popular.

Golden Gate Fortune Cookies Co.

56 Ross Alley

Today Ross Alley is famous for the Golden Gate Fortune Cookies Co., where the only remaining old-fashioned fortune cookie machine in Chinatown is still use. This is a "must-see" for tourists.

With the popularity of Chinese dining came the fortune cookie. Like "*chop suey*," no one knows when it was introduced into Chinatown. Both the Chinese and Japanese take credit. Thus the legend of the Chinese fortune cookie crumbles.

Jennifer B. Lee, in her article in the *New York Times* (1/16/08), reported the researcher in Japanese confectioneries Yasuko Nakamachi uncovered an 1878 book illustrating a man attending multiple round iron molds with long handles resting on a rectangular grill over a bed of charcoal, much like the way fortune cookies were made for generations by small family bakeries near the Shinto shrine outside Kyoto, Japan.

Confectionery shop owners Gary Ono of the Benkyodo Co. (founded 1906) and Brian Kito of Fugetsu-do of Los Angeles (founded 1903) both claim their grandfathers introduced the fortune cookie to America. Erik Hagiware-Nagata mentioned his grandfather Makato Hagiware made the cookie at the Japanese Tea Garden in Golden Gate Park. The daughter of David Jung claims her father made the cookie at their Hong Kong Noodle Co. founded in 1906 in Los Angeles.

At one hundred years old, Eva Lim remembered that while visiting the Tea Garden in the

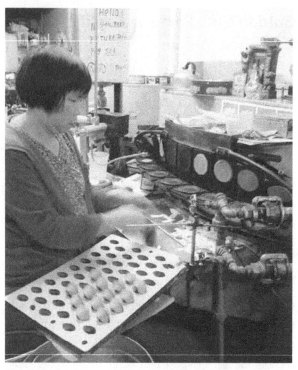

Fortune cookies being molded at Golden Gate Fortune Cookies Co.

1920s, her father bought her a package of the cookies but they were flat, not folded, without the fortune. She was fascinated watching a woman baking the cookies with two waffle-like irons through the window of a market at the northeast corner of Dupont and Pacific Avenue.

Originally the batter was baked in individual molds made in Japan and the cookie was folded by hand when it hardened. The late dentist Dr. Gene Poon described his father's home operation in the early 1930s, with some seven to ten electrically heated units set in a U-shaped assembly line. Each unit was like a waffle iron with two round castings.

During World War II, his father, Bing Cheong Poon, went to work in the shipyard but continued making cookies at night. Gene used to deliver them to Fong Fong Bakery (established 1937), Eastern Bakery (established 1924), and the sidewalk stalls.

Apparently in Chinatown, fortune cookies were a homemade commodity until the mechanized carousal machine was invented by the Japanese and manufactured in Los Angeles.* Kay Heung Noodle Co. on Beckett Alley (founded 1933) by Charles and Harry Soo Hoo used such a machine, which had multiple molds placed in a roughly seven-foot-diameter circle. Workers sat outside the circle, individually picked the soft pliable cookie, and folded in the fortune. Eastern Bakery bought the machine and began to make its own cookies in 1940.

Coming to America in 1952, Franklin Yee worked for ten years before saving enough money to go into business for himself. Yee started his Golden Gate Fortune Cookies Co. in 1962, when most existing fortune cookie bakeries had already switched to a completely automatic system. Lacking funds, Yee stayed with the old-fashioned machine. He remembers clearly that in his initial operation, his sales were only $5.00 a day. From this humble beginning, he turned the business into a main tourist attraction.

How and when the Japanese fortune cookie became the Chinese fortune cookie remains a mystery but it is clear the Chinese made the cookie famous.

---

* Filmmaker Derek Shimoda in his DVD *The Killing of a Chinese Cookie* (2008).

Chee Kung Tong
36 Spofford Alley

In Chinese, the word "Tong" means a meeting hall. For example, a church is called "*Lai By Tong*," meaning "Sunday meeting hall." But in America, the word "Tong" came to mean secret societies notorious for their illegal activities—gang wars, prostitution, gambling, and opium—that plagued the Chinese community for over half a century. The *Chee Kung Tong* (Chinese Freemasons) was founded in San Francisco in 1853 and incorporated in 1879, with chapters established throughout Chinese American communities. This modest three-story brick building is noted not so much for its architectural design as for its historical significance. In China, Chee Kung Tong was a branch of the Triad Secret Society founded to overthrow the Manchu government (1644-1911) and restore Chinese rule. In California, the Chee Kung Tong degenerated into criminal activities, competing with other secret societies to control prostitution and gambling.

Chee Kung Tong returned to its lofty political ideology in 1900 when both Kang Yu-wei's Reform Party and Sun Yat-sen's Revolutionary Party sought its assistance. Originally the Chee Kung Tong supported Kang Yu Wei, but as Dr. Sun's ideology gained popularity, the Chee Kung Tong switched allegiance. When in 1904 immigration officials did not allow entry to Sun, the leader of the Chee Kung Tong, Wong Sam Ark, and the Tong's attorney Oliver Stidger, along with Reverend Ng Poon Chew and Reverend Soo Hoo Nam Art, worked success-

Chee Kung Tong.

fully for his release. Sun stayed at the Chee Kung Tong headquarters and used the society's newspaper, the *Chinese Free Press*, to propagandize his revolutionary cause. Accompanied by Wong Sam Ark, Dr. Sun went on a nationwide tour to generate support and contributions.

When the revolution broke out in China on October 10, 1911, the Chee Kung Tong at 36 Spofford Alley became a distribution point for two million republican government bonds. On November 5, 1911, Chinatown celebrated the establishment of the Republic of China. Atop the roof, the dragon flags of the Manchu government were taken down and the flags of the New Republic were hoisted.

Tien Hou Temple
Sue Hing Benevolent Association
125-29 Waverly Place

The Tien Hou Temple is located on the top floor of the building. *Tien Hou*, the Queen of Heaven and Goddess of the Seven Seas, is the Chinese name for Waverly Place. The owners of the temple claim it is the oldest in San Francisco, established in 1853.

Tien Hou Temple on the top floor.

Tien Hou Temple in the 1890s.

Reports of a Tien Hou Temple at 33 Waverly Place during the 1890s likely refer to the same one. The temple was closed for many years, until 1975, when it reopened due to resurgence of interest from a new immigrant population.

The ground-floor façade of this building has been remodeled using an aluminum sash for the window of the central storefront. The façade of the levels above remains intact with its ornate features. The second floor has a simple iron balcony: brick-work surrounds the area of the three symmetrically placed double-hung windows. The third floor is enlivened by a deeper balcony, with two cast-iron columns and a central doorway framed by a marble surround engraved with Chinese characters and fringed by a band of egg and dart design. The balcony of the temple on the top floor has lotus-shaped metal lanterns, incense pots, shrines, and placard stands as well as two columns and an engraved marble arch around the doorway.

Ning Yung Benevolent Association
41 Waverly Place

The Ning Yung Benevolent Association, comprised of immigrants from Toishan, was founded in 1853 when it separated from its parent organization, the Sze Yup Company. The new association purchased a site at 517 Broadway, behind Adler Place, to build their new headquarters. The association remained on Broadway until in the late 1880s, when it purchased the site on Waverly Place and constructed new headquarters, including a temple to patronize Kwan Kung, the God of War. After the 1906 quake, a new building replaced the old one on the same location.

Embracing the spirit of Americanization, and contrary to the movement to create a new "Oriental City," the association instructed its architect to design its building strictly in keeping with Western architecture, without Oriental embellishments. The temple, dedicated to Kwan Kung, was not included in the new plans.

On October 26, 1907, the association held an open house for their new four-story brick building, followed by a banquet at the Suey Far Low on Jackson Street. That evening at the banquet, President Jow Doong Tarm gave a stirring speech insisting that greater Chinatown must be in keeping with greater San Francisco. Alas, cultural identity proved to be too deeply rooted to overcome. In the 1940s, a false canopy was added across the face of the building, above the second-story windows, simulating a Chinese roof.

Ning Yung Benevolent Association.

(See Kong Chow Benevolent Association.)

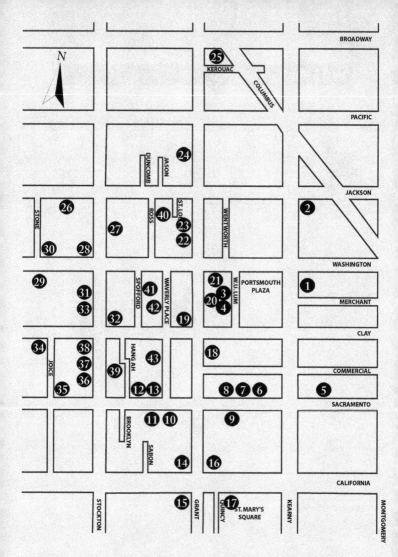

1 Chinese Culture Center
2 Manilatown & I-Hotel
3 Chinese Congregational Church
4 Wing Sang Mortuary
4 Everybody's Bookstore
4 Chinese for Affirmative Action
5 Chy Lung Bazaar
6 Chung Sai Yat Po
7 Chinese Chamber of Commerce
8 Yeong Wo Benevolent Association Building
9 Nam Kue School
10 Chinese Daily Post

11 Chinese Young Men's Christian Association (YMCA)
12 Willie "Woo Woo" Wong Playground
13 Chinese Baptist Church
14 Sing Chong
15 Sing Fat
16 Old St. Mary's Church
17 St. Mary's Square
18 The Chinese World
19 Soo Yuen Benevolent Association
20 Loong Kong Tien Yee Association
21 Chinese Telephone Exchange

Main Tour

The core of Chinatown is a historic district replete with landmarks that trace the development of the neighborhood from the City's earliest days to the present. Begin the tour from Portsmouth Plaza with No. 1 through No. 43 and you will discover the realities of the history of the City's oldest surviving ethnic neighborhood. From City Lights, walk on Columbus Avenue to Kearny Street toward Portsmouth Plaza. This tour will take the whole day, depending on your depth of interest. For those with limited time, the following short tours are suggested. Feel free to wander and explore yourself. I assure you, there are no secret underground tunnels—never were and never will be.

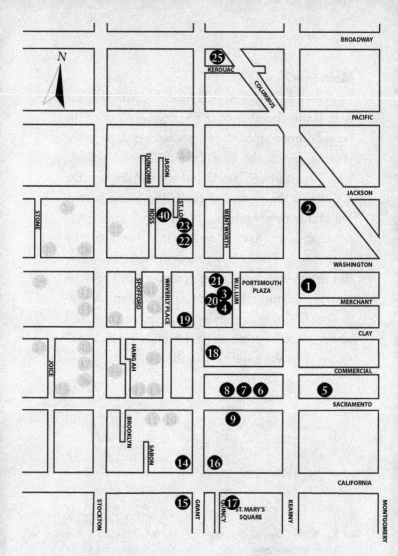

Short Tour No. 1
Portsmouth Plaza, Sacramento Street, and Grant Avenue.

Following the numbers on the map, begin your tour from Portsmouth Plaza, walk south on Kearny onto Sacramento, thence to Grant Avenue, and from California, walk northward to Jackson Street. If time permits, take side trips along the way onto Washington Street to site No. 21, the original Chinese Telephone Company and the location of the first San Francisco newspaper published by Sam Brannan. Continue back to Grant and walk to Jackson. Turn uphill onto Jackson Street and note adjacent alleyways with their own Chinese names. Stop by Ross Alley and visit No. 40, the fortune cookie bakery. (Tour 1 may be combined with tour 2 or tour 3.)

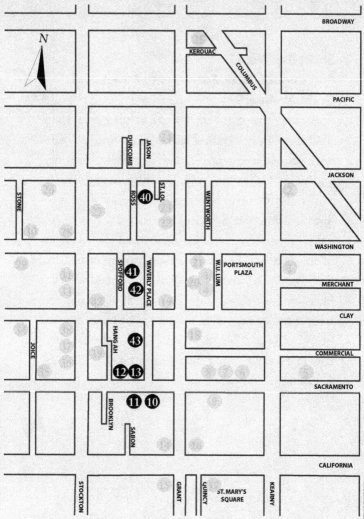

Short Tour No. 2
Ross, Spofford, Waverly Place

Walk through Ross, cross Washington to Spofford, and stop at site No. 41, Chee Kung Tong. Continue through Spofford to Waverly. Observe the architecture on the buildings on the west side of the street, which makes eclectic use of classic design elements intermixed with Chinese colors to create the illusion of a Chinese streetscape. Climb three flights of stairs to No. 42, the Tien Hou Temple; stop by site No. 43, the Ning Yung Building. If time permits, continue on toward Sacramento Street and stop at No. 13 Baptist Church, No. 10 *Chinese Daily Post*, No. 11 Chinese YMCA, and No. 12 "Woo Woo" Wong Playground.

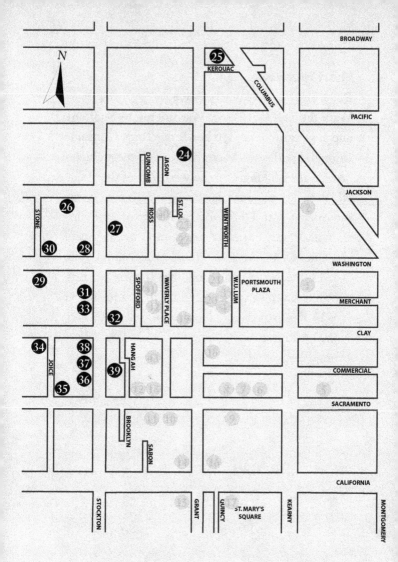

Short Tour No. 3
Stockton Street

From Waverly Street, walk uphill toward Stockton Street. Within Stockton Street lies the complex social, political, and cultural milieu that is Chinatown. Traditional "old world" culture of the East stands juxtaposed with the churches of the West, symbols of assimilation. Take a side trip up Clay Street to No. 34, the YWCA building, now the Chinese Historical Society of America. This museum is highly recommended. A modest admission fee is charged. Visit No. 35 Cameron House, proceed downhill back onto Stockton, head north to Washington then uphill on Washington and visit No. 29 Gordon Elementary School and No. 30 the Gum Moon Residence. Return to Stockton and continue north and visit No. 27 the Chinese American Citizens Alliance; continue northward to Jackson, then uphill and visit No. 26 the Chinese Hospital. Walk through Washington to Pacific and compete with locals for a true shopping experience. See live fish, crabs, and lobsters just as your grandparents had in their days. Continue down Pacific, head North onto Grant to Kerouac Alley to City Lights on Columbus Avenue.

Works Cited

Asbury, Herbert. 1933. *The Barbary Coast: An Informal History of the San Francisco Underworld*. NY: Alfred A. Knopf.

Barry, T.A. and B.A. Patten. 1949. *San Francisco, California, 1850*. Oakland, California: Biobooks.

Brown, John Henry. 1933. *Reminiscences and Incidents of the Early Days of San Francisco 1845-50*. San Francisco: The Grabhorn Press.

Condit, Ira M. 1900. *The Chinaman as We See Him, and Fifty Years of Work for Him*. Chicago, New York, Toronto: Fleming H. Revell Co.

Cowles, Colin Barrett. 1989. *The Loong Kong Tien Yee Association of San Francisco, An Account of Its Origins, History, and Evolution*. Author's collection.

Gibson, Otis. 1877. *The Chinese in America*. Cincinnati, Ohio: Hitchcock & Walden.

Hunt, Rockwell D. 1950. *California's Stately Hall of Fame*. Stockton, California: College of the Pacific.

Hunter, W.C. 1965. *The "Fan Kwae" at Canton Before Treaty Days 1825-1844*. Taipei: Ch'eng-wen Publishing Co.

Kwan, Florence C. 1973. "Christian Leaders of Yesteryear" in *The Chinese Congregational Church 100th Anniversary*. Author's collection.

McKinley, Edward H. 1986. *Marching to Glory: The History of the Salvation Army in the United States, 1880-1980*. 2nd ed. Atlanta, GA: Salvation Army Supplies.

Quincy, Josiah. 1847. *The Journals of Major Samuel Shaw*. Boston, Massachusetts: Wm. Crosby and H.P. Nichols.

San Francisco Daily Morning Call. 1889.

Smith, Carl T. 1969. "The Gillespie Brothers: Early Links Between Hong Kong and California." *Chung Chi Bulletin*.

Smith, Carl T. 1985. *Chinese Christians: Elites, Middlemen, and the Church in Hong Kong*. Hong Kong, Oxford, New York: Oxford University Press.

Taylor, Bayard. 1850. *Eldorado: Adventures in the Path of Empire*. Vol. 1. NY: George P. Putman, London: Richard Bentley.

Selected Bibliography

Bancroft, Hubert Howe. *The New Pacific*. New York: The Bancroft Company, 1915, 3rd revised ed.

Bau, Mingchien Joshua. *The Open Door Doctrine in Relation to China*. New York: The Macmillan Co., 1923.

Chapman, Charles E. *A History of California: The Spanish Period*. New York: The Macmillan Company, 1921.

Chinn, Thomas, H. Mark Lai, and Philip P. Choy. *A History of the Chinese in California: A Syllabus*. San Francisco Chinese Historical Society of America, 1969.

Choy, Philip P., Lorraine Dong, and Marlon, Hom. *The Coming Man: 19th Century American Perceptions of the Chinese*. Hong Kong: Joint Publishing Co. Ltd., 1994.

Cleland, Robert Glass. *A History of California: The American Period*. New York: The Macmillan Company, 1926.

Coolidge, Mary Elizabeth. *Chinese Immigration*. New York: Henry Holt and Co., 1909.

Cross, Ira B. *A History of the Labor Movement in California*. Berkeley: University of California Press, 1935.

Dennett, Tyler. *Americans in Eastern Asia: A Critical Study of the Policy of the United States with Reference to China, Japan and Korea in the 19th Century*. New York: The Macmillan Company, 1922.

Fleming, Sandford. *God's Gold: The Story of Baptist Beginnings in California, 1849-1860*. Philadelphia: The Judson Press, 1949.

Greenbie, Sydney and Marjorie. *Gold of Ophir or the Lure that Made America*. Garden City, New York: Doubleday, Page & Company, 1925.

Habal, Estella. *San Francisco's International Hotel*. Philadelphia: Temple University Press.

Harlow, Neal. *The Maps of San Francisco Bay from the Spanish Discovery in 1769 to the American Occupation*. San Francisco: The Book Club of California, 1950.

Layton, Thomas N. *Gifts from the Celestial Kingdom*. Palo Alto, CA: Stanford University Press, 2002.

Layton, Thomas N. *The Voyage of the Frolic*. Palo Alto, CA: Stanford University Press, 1997.

Liu, Michael, Kim Geron, and Tracy Lai. *The Snake Dance of Asian American Activism*. Lanham, MD: Lexington Books, 2008.

Louie, Steve and Glenn Omatsu, eds. *Asian American: The Movement and the Moment*. Los Angeles: UCLA Asian American Studies Center Press, 2001.

Ma, L. Eve Armentrout. *Revolutionaries, Monarchist,s and Chinatowns: Chinese Politics in the Americas and the 1911 Revolution*. Honolulu, HI: University of Hawaii Press, 1990.

McKee, Delber L. *Chinese Exclusion Versus the Open Door Policy, 1900-1906: Clashes Over China Policy in the Roosevelt Era*. Detroit, MI: Wayne University Press, 1977.

O'Connor, Richard. *Pacific Destiny: An Informal History of the U.S. in the Far East: 1776-1968*. Boston, Toronto: Little, Brown and Company, 1969.

Phillips, Catherine Coffin. *Portsmouth Plaza*. San Francisco: John Henry Nash, 1932.

Pond, William C. *Gospel Pioneering: Reminiscences of Early Congregationalism in California, 1838-1920*. Oberlin, Ohio: Press of the News Printing, 1921.

Riggs, Fred W. *Pressures on Congress: A Study of the Repeal of Chinese Exclusion*. New York: King's Crown Press, 1950.

Rubinstein, Murray A. *The Origins of the Anglo-American Missionary Enterprise in China*. Lanham, MD and London: The Scarecrow Press, Inc., 1996.

Saxton, Alexander. *The Indispensable Enemy: Labor and the Anti-Chinese Movement in California*. Berkeley, Los Angeles, and London: University of California Press, 1971.

Soule, Frank, John H. Gihon, and James Nisbet. *The Annals of San Francisco*. New York, San Francisco, London: D. Appleton & Company, 1855.